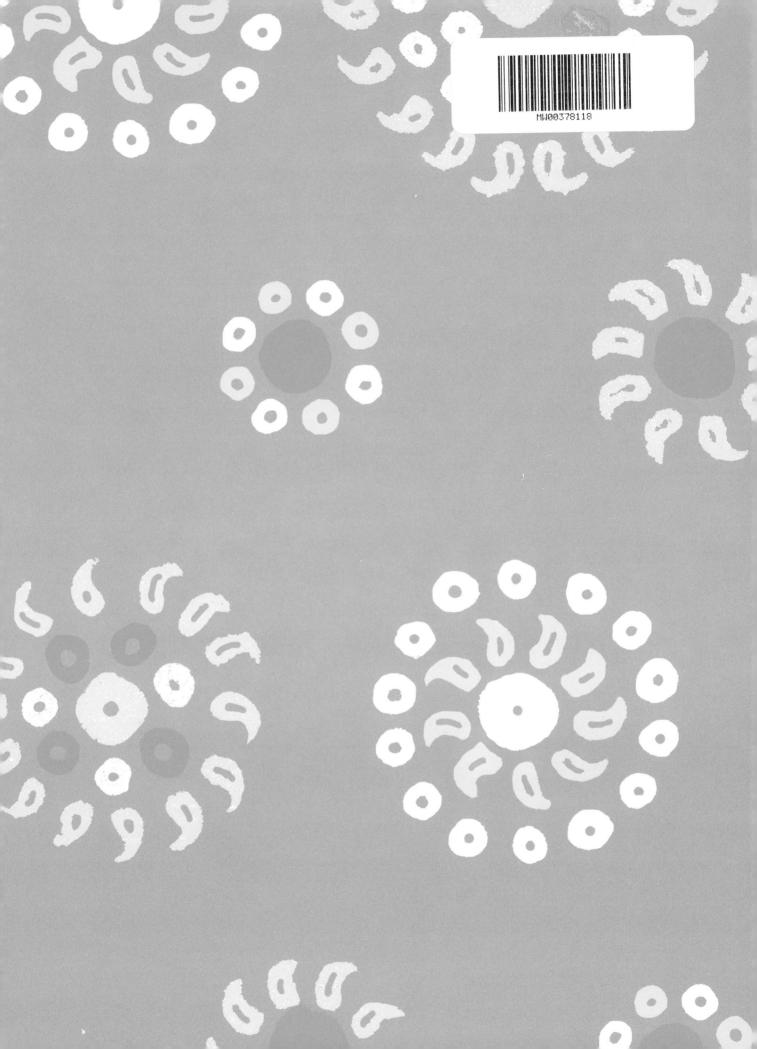

Creating a Home

KATHRYN M. IRELAND

Creating a Home

Foreword by Marc Appleton

GIBBS SMITH
TO ENRICH AND INSPIRE HUMANKIND

Salt Lake City | Charleston | Santa Fe | Santa Barbara

First Edition
13 12 11 10   5 4 3 2

Published by
Gibbs Smith
P.O. Box 667
Layton, Utah 84041

1.800.835.4993 orders
www.gibbs-smith.com

Design by Debra McQuiston and Kathryn M. Ireland
Printed and bound in China
Gibbs Smith books are printed on either recycled, 100% post-consumer waste,
FSC-certified papers or on paper produced from a 100% certified sustainable
forest/controlled wood source.

Library of Congress Cataloging-in-Publication Data

Ireland, Kathryn M.
 Creating a home / Kathryn M. Ireland ; foreword by Marc Appleton. — 1st ed.
   p. cm.
 ISBN-13: 978-1-4236-0595-9
 ISBN-10: 1-4236-0595-0
 1. Ireland, Kathryn M.—Themes, motives. 2. Interior decoration—California—Ojai. 3.
Architecture, Domestic—Conservation and restoration—California—Ojai. I. Title.
 NK2004.3.I73A4 2009
 747—dc22
                        2009017198

To my mother, Lillian,
who let me paint my bedroom
emerald green and throw
shocking pink scatter pillows
on the living room sofa.

Contents

Architect

Foreword by Marc Appleton

Like many other financially successful tycoons from New England and the Midwest, Edward Drummond Libbey, who had turned a small family glass company in Toledo, Ohio, into the industrial giant Libbey-Owens-Ford, ventured to Southern California in search of a second home in a more temperate winter climate. Since first visiting it in 1908, he had taken a shine to the Ojai Valley, a picturesque agricultural community east of Ventura, eventually purchased a significant amount of real estate there, and in 1914 proceeded to develop his vision for rebuilding the town of Ojai as a romantic Spanish Colonial Village.

Libbey was already acquainted with the more established architects practicing in Southern California and had hired some of them for various projects, including Myron Hunt and Elmer Grey, George Washington Smith and Richard Requa, who assisted Libbey in planning and redesigning downtown Ojai into the architectural center it is today. Wallace Neff, a young Pasadena architect who had opened an office in Ojai a year after acquiring his license in 1921, may have been the new guy on the block, but Libbey hired him in 1923 to design the Ojai Valley Country Club and Hotel and, while he was at it, a stable building for Libbey's own estate.

Neff's architectural bent, no doubt encouraged by his client's enthusiasm and vision, tended toward a regional but eclectic aesthetic. The design for the stables in particular, although rustically Mediterranean, also owes a debt to some French farm fantasy. The adobe structure is definitely a utilitarian, vernacular building, but it is whimsically inspired as well by something out of the French countryside. As one can readily see from the original plan and photos that were published in 1924, this brand new building suggested a kitschy spirit that was working hard to convince us that

it might have descended from pioneering immigrant farmers from France who had settled in Ojai decades ago.

When one adds eighty years of age to the original building, including the subsequent remodeling and additions to the compound designed by the architect Austen Pierpont in the 1930s, and several eventual occupations by people rather than farm animals who were now making the stables their home, it is easy to accept that by the time designer Kathryn Ireland finally saw it in 2003, the property had indeed acquired some real history as a regional landmark. The fact that it was a bit of a shambles when she encountered it only added to its appeal. And so the stables began yet another life under the designer's direction, but this was not to be the typical renovation.

One of the inevitable characteristics of most projects designed by professionals (and this appears to have been true of the original Neff product) is that they are neatly finished—they are of a piece, in a word, "done." Often they are so perfectly complete that one's soul cannot enter in. There are no fissures or cracks, no worn surfaces or rough spots that would make one feel they could trespass comfortably and make it

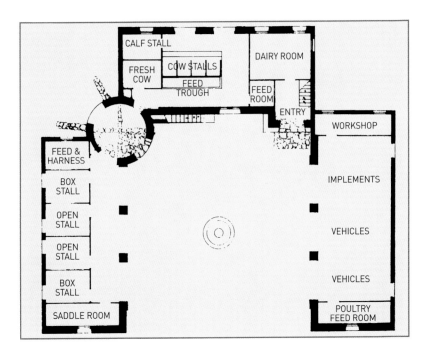

theirs. Kathryn Ireland is not of this school. She revels in the rough spots. If you have ever been privileged to visit her home in the South of France near Montauban, you can instantly appreciate her aesthetic inclinations. Her farmhouse there, like the Libbey stables, was a ruin when she found it, and, although much more marvelously comfy and functional now after her makeover, its great attraction and accomplishment, ironically, is that it is still a bit of a ruin. Kathryn has that rarest of abilities to know when to leave well enough alone and savor rather than despair the thing that is not quite finished.

When Kathryn first called me to look at a property she had found for sale in Ojai, I was doubtful. There are times when I imagine my friend was born into the wrong era. She always seems unreasonably ebullient, keen and excited about many things the rest of us take for granted. Although I pretend always to join in her Gatsby-esque enthusiasm (how can one not?), I secretly maintain a healthy skepticism nurtured, perhaps, by too many years of architectural practice. Kathryn often seems like a giraffe with her head gliding through the treetops while the rest of us intently scan the ground at our feet for impediments. So when I first saw the Libbey property, it appeared to be not only a ruin but an incredibly impracti-

cal, money pit of a ruin that would take too much time, effort, bureaucratic negotiating and dollars to salvage. I advised her accordingly and suggested a healthier alternative would be for her to get over her fixation for the ruin's prospects and move on to an easier opportunity.

Something else I am always learning about Kathryn, however, is never to underestimate her stubbornness once she gets hold of an idea. The combination is an anatomical stretch, but, low and behold, there is a bulldog inside that giraffe! As I consider now what she has accomplished with the place, happily presented in the pages of this book, I must question altogether my initial skepticism and can't help but cheer her forward to the next seemingly impossible or impractical challenge.

I also realize that a significant characteristic of her special talent is being able to recognize that a part of the design challenge is to leave some of it undone. When she refers to the attractions of "the worn ruin" or "the patina of age and use," these are not the usual aesthetic pretensions towards some nostalgically perfect re-creation of age but the rough and tumble facts of our lives, which usually work against perfection. Perhaps it is her experience raising three sons; perhaps it is her own nomadic background or her festively impatient spirit. Whatever it is, she knows that not all designed houses are homes, and we are grateful and full of admiration for what she does (or undoes) and how she does (or undoes) it. Very few people in her industry have her innate understanding of why it matters to celebrate history with all its imperfections, and that interior design, like cosmetic surgery, can be a risky business when perfection is the predominant goal.

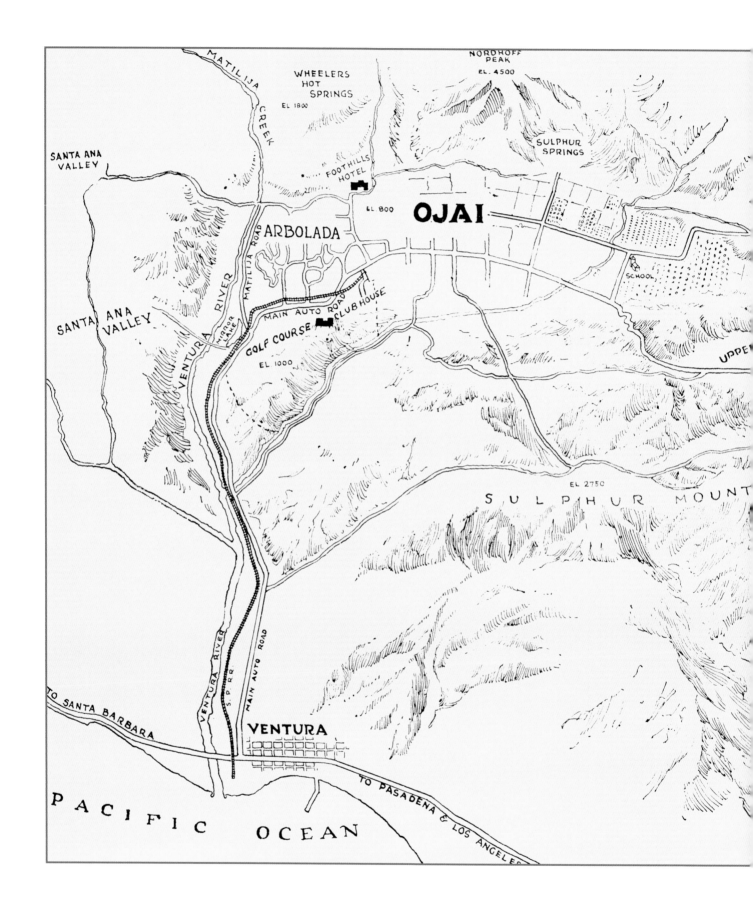

TOPA TOPA
MOUNTAINS
EL. 6351

LLEY

Introduction
& History
of the Libbey Ranch

I love a good ruin. Whether it's a sagging barn, a broken bicycle, a jilted bachelor, or a curdled bearnaise, bringing something spoiled back to life has given me great satisfaction and pleasure from very early childhood. Well-mended Coalport porcelain, imaginatively resewn Irish tabletop linens, and reinhabited stone fishermen's cottages with brightly painted shutters continue to give me great joy all these years later.

Europeans may have learned to esteem and romanticize these relics out of necessity, as there have certainly been periods of war and economic turmoil when replacement or acquisition of anything new was simply out of the question. Regardless, character is destiny, and I find myself still gravitating towards almost anything vintage, anything that proudly bears the patina of age and use. My own preference for the old over the new has never stood in the way of living a gracious, efficient, convenient lifestyle in the modern world. I think that "splitting the difference" between, say, hundred-year-old side chairs and a trestle table of recycled Douglas fir is a much more evolved and graceful design solution than either "period paralysis" or "city new" design schemes.

mising period authenticity, style, and structural integrity; to convert the house into a functional home for everyday living, for life today. I will look at an old stone and stucco pile far from the Dordogne and see a perfectly nonchalant weekend home of uneven flooring and variable ceiling heights, but with excellent lighting throughout, a tip-top kitchen and a lot of irreproducible charm. While post-WW II construction in America consists of quickly erected suburban ranch houses, in contrast, a European's innate drift is toward conservation and restoration. As for my obsession, Don Quixote said it right, "The proof of the pudding is in the eating." And this was certainly the through line of my love affair with the charmingly ruined stunner of a property

I think that "splitting the difference" between, say, hundred-year-old side chairs and a trestle table of recycled Douglas fir is a much more evolved and graceful design solution than either "period paralysis" or "city new" design schemes.

As a natural outgrowth of my practice in interior design, I often found myself terribly immersed in the construction process, retrofitting the electrical and plumbing in addition to stripping and refinishing crown moldings and door hardware. I have earned my stripes as a partisan on the side of "sympathetic restoration" both in the United States and Europe.

The challenge here is to divine the line between functionality and fetishism and then walk it—to modernize outdated building support systems without compro-

in Southern California's Ojai Valley—the Libbey Ranch.

Though I have made career marks in the field of restoration, I have never consciously gone on the hunt for a house to "fix up." But on a cold day a few Januarys ago, I was idly going through the *L.A. Times* Real Estate section when a photograph of an early-twentieth-century Spanish Revival estate in a rather sad and dilapidated state leapt off the page. Rescuing ruins is a form of religion for me and this *was* a Sunday.

The house was originally designed in the

Above: The clean slate before any work began. The old carriage house converted to kitchen had great bones: existing terra-cotta floors, an extraordinary fireplace, and French doors opening onto the courtyard. **Below:** The Basque chandelier, shaded in parchment and barely visible here, was an important focal point in the great room and original to the house. The tile staircase leading to the mezzanine had exceptional iron balustrades and original Talavera tile.

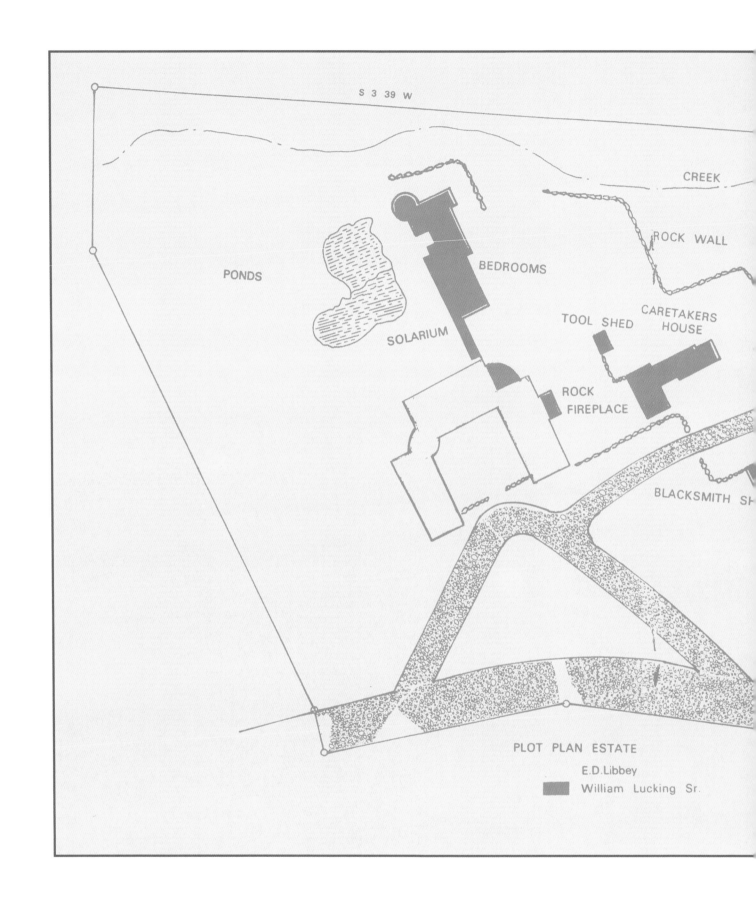

S 3 39 W

CREEK

ROCK WALL

CARETAKERS
HOUSE

TOOL SHED

BEDROOMS

PONDS

SOLARIUM

ROCK
FIREPLACE

BLACKSMITH SH

PLOT PLAN ESTATE

E.D. Libbey

William Lucking Sr.

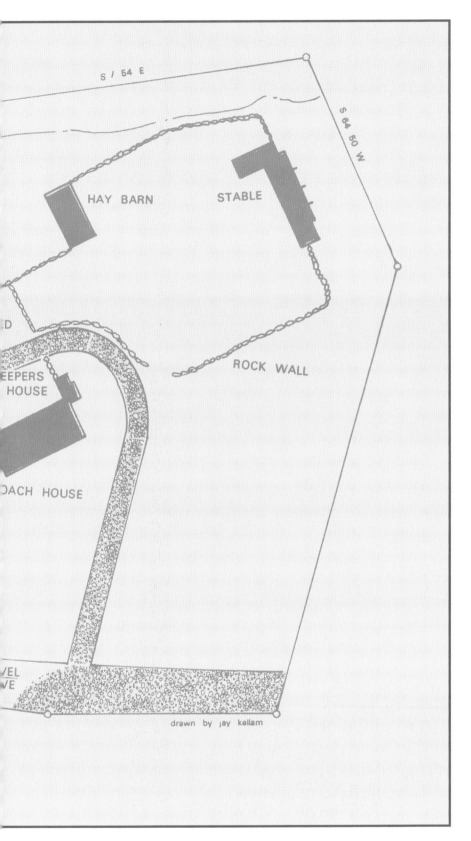

S / 54 E

S 64 50 W

HAY BARN

STABLE

EEPERS
HOUSE

ROCK WALL

OACH HOUSE

VEL
VE

drawn by jay kellam

early 1920s by renowned Pasadena architect Wallace Neff as a dairy barn and stable for glass magnate Edward Drummond Libbey of Toledo, Ohio. After Libbey's death, the property was purchased by a Detroit-based lawyer for the Ford Motor Company, William Lucking, Sr., who hired local architect Austen Pierpont to reconceive the barn and outbuildings as a residential compound for use as a holiday home. It was to be a folly, a place to entertain his friends and family.

Having lived in Los Angeles for almost half my life, to discover this little charming oasis one county north was exhilarating. The only direction I ever really go is south, to the airport so I can hop on a plane and head back to Europe. And here on my doorstep was this extraordinary place, funky and unpretentious, with its photogenic arrangement of mountain ranges, rolling oak-covered hills, flatlands, avocado ranches and the swirling, intoxicating aroma of oranges. Though Ojai lacks commanding views of the Pacific, the secluded enclave is only fifteen miles inland from the coast and a one hour and fifteen minute drive from downtown Los Angeles.

The private road that leads to the property is very unassuming, in keeping with my taste. The instant you pass through two sets of gates, you're in your own world. With the majestic Topa Topa peaks standing guard at one end and green meadows flanking the other, the enveloping landscape still holds its strong, rugged qualities and maintains an illusion of vast wildness.

I've never seen anything quite like this property. A mixture of adobe, wood, and river rock, the primary residence and the

In all likelihood, nothing had been maintained at this property for very nearly thirty years. There was so much deferred maintenance to be redressed, and more was discovered as my crew made preliminary reconnaissances into wall chaseways, crawl spaces, junction boxes, and chimneys. Obviously, the sequencing of the various components of the restoration would be contingent upon the reconfigurations that I was contemplating for some of the rooms.

several outbuildings—including a charming carriage house, entrance lodge, stable block, and guest cottages—all combined to create a compound very reminiscent of the San Ysidro Ranch or somewhere tucked away up in Napa. Situated on 7.5 acres, the various buildings were well laid out and gave the property a feeling of deep and expansive space. Despite (or perhaps because of) the overgrown cacti and shaggy stands of California oaks and eucalyptuses, the rambling estate still exemplified the unpretentious grandeur of Old California style.

My immediate thought was that if you took my farm in France and my house in Santa Monica and tossed them into a blender, it would spew out this house.

ship were redesigned to serve as communal living areas. Apart from the courtyard in front, there was no uniformity in terms of style or symmetry.

The realtor was down on it. He explained that it had been languishing on the MLS for a few years and that by now the brokerage community was lukewarm because the buildings themselves clearly required extensive renovation. If the property had been located in Montecito, it would probably be easier to visualize an exit strategy for a prospective buyer but harder to do in hippie Ojai.

Once inside the 5,000- square-foot primary residence, I saw right away that it was a pure, good space. The interior was

My immediate thought was that if you took
my farm in France and my house in Santa Monica and tossed
them into a blender, it would spew out this house.

Reminiscent of the barns in France that I live in, this idiosyncratic architecture combines the best elements of Spanish Colonial Revival, French country (with punctuation of Norman detailing), and casual barn living. In the tradition of Spanish architectural creations in California, there were walls of original adobe brick, flagstone terraces, deep-set windows, arched doorways and liberal use of wrought iron. A balcony constructed of rough wood spanning the front of the structure and the roof of hand-split wood shakes suggested the adobe dwellings of early California. The main residence was U-shaped, with a circular tower connecting two wings that under Lucking's steward-

distinguished by heavy wood lintels, interior beams, cool white adobe walls and wood flooring of original thick red oak planks. The showstopper was the great room: with its two-story height and arched beam ceiling, this grand living room had originally been used as a cow shed. A formal fireplace dominated one end, a large balcony overlooking the living area the other. The wrought-iron staircase leading to the balcony and alcove loft had colorful, kaleidoscopic Mexican tiles of a different design on each of the risers. A massive iron chandelier with parchment shades was the perfect centerpiece for the great and gorgeous space.

The adjacent carriage shed had been transformed into a combination kitchen and casual family dining area. Not as formal as the main great room, this room was centered around a massive rock fireplace, the opening of which was large enough to learn to love all manner of flaws in geometry, finish and coloration. None of these original Spanish Colonial Revival residences come with regular floor plans or crisply edged rooms or evened floors or uniform ceiling height. This is an architecture

accommodate a table and two chairs, creating a warm and romantic nook.

In the absence of any one truly indigenous style, Lucking had simply determined that the residence should incorporate and marry all of those attributes he had most admired on a summer tour around England, France, and Spain in the mid-twenties.

Anyone like me who loves ruins must style that was really forced to embrace and perhaps even celebrate irregularity, which then became part and parcel of its comfort and charm. Yes, you'll find archways that look semicircular, but upon closer inspection they are not really true, just good approximations. You will find seemingly uniformly tiled floors but then discover that the "uniformity" is simply an optical

"There is a gutsiness about Kathryn's design
work that embraces anti-perfectionism . . . but in reality,
she orchestrated every detail . . . to make
everything look and feel natural and organic."

—Peter Dunham, designer

illusion created by the randomly laid flooring upon essentially leveled floors. Overhead, the timber used as rafters and beams and in the doors and window frames was only roughly similar. More fastidious designers would likely have made a concerted effort to square off these rooms and re-level these floors and true up the staircases and ledges. Southern California is a living testimony to the tug-of-war between the rustic and irregular and the rectilinear and bourgeois, between the Latin and the Yankee. Though an Anglo-Saxon by birth, I find myself very much on the side of the romantic, relic-loving Mediterranean culture of irregularity.

As I swooned, I could sense the terrible amount of deferred maintenance. Of course, the house had been admired—so many Hollywood celebrities had been seriously interested but had reluctantly passed as the place was much, much more than a fixer-upper; it was determined too daunting a job even for movie star architecture junkies with very deep pockets. As it was built as a barn and then in the thirties adapted into a living space, it was never designed as a traditional home. It therefore had limitations to the bulk of prospective buyers. If you had small children, it wasn't ideal; the

layout was too eccentric for a family with conventional tastes. But for me, the house was too good to be true.

The "diamond in the rough" is a time immemorial hook for those of us who live to breathe new life into a neglected or overlooked object. The thrill of bringing one's skill set to bear on something the market isn't valuing is priceless. There is no substitute for the personal satisfaction of polishing tarnished silver or removing lime.

The Libbey Ranch was just waiting to be loved and restored. Although the owner couldn't have been a lovelier woman and had kept it up as best she could, it was very much a second home for her, and I well know what a big financial commitment it is to keep a place like this going.

I knew that I had to have the Libbey Ranch because I began having nightmares about skylights in the great room and the buildings being torn down. I started imagining myriad plausible scenarios whereby I could afford it. I could sell all my houses and move my design studio to Ojai; I could consolidate my professional and personal lives by bundling them together, leading the life I love in France and at home in California. I could get up early to ride my temporarily jet-lagged horses before the daily tasks

"You'd be surprised how easy it is to ruin a ruin."

—Kathryn M. Ireland

of cutting fabric and following up on tile orders. The seller was motivated and so was I. I decided to put in a crazy offer and see what happened.

As an idea, my plan was perfect! But reality was another story. For my three teenage boys, happily ensconced in Santa Monica at school and with friends, this was not an option. No pile of bricks was so important as to make my kids unhappy. But I still had to save this house. It wasn't a listed building but in my opinion it was historically important, one of Neff's earliest works. When the realtor started saying people were interested in it for land value, I ultimately came up with a solution to buy the house that would enable me to renovate the property and ultimately find the right person to live there and love it. And that's eventually what

happened. Although the house wasn't destined to be mine, I was destined to save it.

Like a marriage, you don't really know what you're getting into when buying a house. You may think that you know a great deal about your intended after a close and careful survey of inspection reports, background checks, and character references, but there is always something you will never have seen coming, never have been able to anticipate or even imagine. Any "house of a certain age" will have untold secrets or discretions that not even the canniest of inspectors can reveal. At the Libbey Ranch, I did know that there was a good roof in place—a large plus, as the roof area was considerable. But the day escrow closed and we took ownership of the ranch, all of the toilets backed up. It was symbolic.

Although the house wasn't destined to be mine, I was destined to save it.

Originally, I had conceived a very straightforward restoration of the main residential building: I was going to update the kitchen with new appliances and fixtures and clean and brighten the existing tiled flooring and beamed ceiling; I was going to replace some of the porcelain fixtures in the bathrooms and subtly retile. I wanted to lightly refinish the original wooden flooring. I could continue to believe that the whole estate simply needed a little dusting and cleaning, so to speak, up until the moment that I broke down and did a little of my own after-the-fact due diligence and tore open my first wall only to find utterly useless wiring. By that time, of course, the affair was fully set in motion and I just decided to roll with each new revelation as if I had expected it all along. One change order necessarily led to another, and soon the scope of work we had envisioned was actually considerably more intensive than any of us had bargained for.

So this, then, is a story of rather impulsive infatuation that matured into a sort of love born of perseverance. It would ultimately come to an end, but my heart isn't really broken. There will be more occasions for breathlessness and dreams. The latest *L.A. Times* Real Estate section is right at hand.

Inspiration

My lifelong passion for traveling the world began at age two when my parents took me to Egypt on holiday. One of my earliest memories is gazing out the window of the Mena House Hotel at the extraordinary pyramids of Giza. The gift of wide and expansive travel is something I chose to provide for my own children. Instead of sending them off to the playing fields of Eton, all three boys went to Santa Monica High and we invested the tuition money in a house in France and trips to exotic and far-flung locations. From the time they were little, their only question to me when the suitcases were being packed was, "How many plane rides, Mom?" They learned early that most great places take more than one ride.

Whenever we travel I am constantly on the prowl for new color stories. Expression of color from country to country can change quite dramatically, and I am always delighted to discover some new combinations. My innate Anglo-Saxon prejudice for cobalt blue on a white field is frequently turned on its head when I find myself in, say, Guatemala, staring at a garish yellow-green-orange combination that seems quite ravishing.

Due to decades of globe-trotting, I've accumulated quite an extensive mental archive of color combinations. At the Libbey Ranch, I found myself going kamikaze with color stories that came out of two entirely disparate equatorial regions—the warm spice notes of North Africa's hard desert landscapes and the pulsating greens, reds, and yellows of the Central American jungles.

Above: A spice merchant at the market in Marrakech. The main square comes to life at sundown. There is nothing more fun than sauntering through and admiring the various food vendors and chefs at work. **Right:** A patchwork rag rug makes colorful attire for this languid creature.

These roofs of the Trullis in Puglia reassured me that the roofs at the Libbey Ranch did not necessarily need to be replaced with red clay tile, the more traditional roofing material for Hispanic architecture in Southern California.

Below: The original fishermen's dwellings in Baltimore, West Cork, have been converted into pubs and pizza parlors. This area has now become one of Ireland's trendy tourist destinations.

Above and Right: A street vendor in La Boca, Buenos Aires. This is the Tango district, where vibrantly colored corrugated tin buildings match the flamboyant costumes of the resident dancers. These loudly decorated tango parlors were at one time demure nineteenth-century residences.

Above: A painted ceiling panel I found in Marrakech along with an outfit for me! **Left:** A brightly colored wooden door in the Souk in Essaouira, Morocco.

Above: A chateau in the Loire Valley demonstrates the long-standing European tradition of leaving well-wrought construction open to the eye. The pale color also reminds me of the stone and river rock found and utilized all over the Libbey Ranch property. **Left:** This fabric, conceived while restoring the house at Ojai, is part of my "Mexico Meets Morocco" collection.

Below: A wall of paintings from Hunt Slonem's Studio in New York. I'm crazy for his bold colors and wildlife paintings.

Above: The combination of pattern and stripes with antique furnishings revived this otherwise long dark corridor at the Greystone Mansion in Beverly Hills. **Left:** A rundown farm building I came across in Ojai. I thought I was somewhere near Segovia, Spain.

THE Great Room

After the naturally magnetic appeal
of the renovated kitchen, the second-
most compelling, most-inspired gathering
place is the room that collects the most
unstructured leisure time of inhabitants
and guests—the living room. The living
room at the ranch was so visually arresting
that we took to calling it the great room.

The real yeoman's journey for me begins with the conception of my vision, incorporating the many distinct portions of the room. Then follow the identification and acquisition of right pieces in style and size that will allow for functional duality, for exhibitionistic and crowded moments as well as discreet and forgotten ones.

This is a process that I start with: a few essential pieces and then the room really starts to speak to me in a way. It is very hard to explain, this process of collaboration with the ghost of an old room, but suffice it to say that it requires some faith and nonlinear problem solving.

The majority of the furniture that eventually found its way into the great room at the ranch was purchased along the brocante circuit in southwest France and some of the best antiques shops (Summerland)

in Southern California, from dealers that I've developed great relationships with over the years. A few of the pieces had been much loved but had washed up as homeless artifacts on the shores of my studio in Santa Monica, along with other furniture and accessories that I knew would one day be perfect for rooms I had yet to lay eyes on. It is always so gratifying to find the perfect home for a long-loved and much moved favorite piece. I was happy to see some of my old friends take up happy residence in this marvelous room.

What emerged via this idiosyncratic, pushmepullyou method of artistic collaboration between ghost and designer was a total success. The great room is equally comfortable hosting cocktails for eighty or sheltering a new couple by the fire. It really never feels too big or too small.

THE DESIGNING

of any large and gracious living area to be both expansive and intimate is always a challenge. First I envisage the grander, more public, purpose of the room and only subsequently try to incorporate those more quiet and private uses—the conversations between old friends, the triumphant finishing of *War and Peace*, the stolen nap, the unexpected tête-à-tête. The great room at the Libbey Ranch lived up to its name with great bones and great character. It was also quite large and had fabulous old-growth wooden floors, full of marring irregularities from decades of use. There was a voluminous vaulted ceiling, again with lovely old dark wooden beams, that added another dimension of grandeur to this horizontally magnificent space. And, then, there were the show-stopping sculpted, tiled and railed staircase along one wall and a gorgeous fireplace dominating another, focusing and anchoring the entire room.

Attending to the refurbishment of the floors, the iron balustrades, the adobe walls and the original electrified sconces was like preparing a canvas. There was not much doubt in my mind about how to set the stage here. I simply reinvigorated what had proven its utility over seventy-odd years.

WHAT FUNCTIONS

as the dining room at the ranch is really just an ambling adjacent extension to what I have taken to calling the great room. The ceiling is much lower here, which not only physically defines the room but also gives it a more cozy feeling. The lower ceiling serves to quiet the space and better contain candlelight, conversation and the convivial aromatic enthusiasms of communally shared food and wine. Natural light is at a minimum at this end of the great room, so daytime use of this space was always likely at a minimum; anything after twilight, however, was an entirely different matter.

I was able to add some fantastic wall sconces that extended the lighting scheme of the great room and that also could be individually adjusted to create exactly that level of intimacy any gathering might call for. Somewhat unorthodox is the fact that the principal front door of the residence opens directly upon this space, forcing this "dining room" to do a bit of double duty as an entry hall/foyer and transitional space. In the end, this arrangement is entirely apt and even convenient as the whole notion of a remote and formally designated dining space has always struck me as inefficient, static and anachronistic. How much livelier to put a little more effort into the use of one's home and move a few chairs around to reconfigure available spaces as needs may demand.

Instead of having perfectly matching, unnecessarily oversized suites of dining room chairs, I used some chairs I had that were smaller, allowing for the addition of extra place settings as my guest list happily grows late in the day. Comfort at the dinner table should not be the paramount concern; all of the "plushness" currently in vogue really just crowds out much of the fun of entertaining. Over meals, one should be pitched forward, involved in merriment and conversation instead of sunk backward into the dark recesses of a 40,000-square-foot chair. I like a chair size that not only complements the proportion of the table but also allows a good number of people to squeeze together. The time has come for oversized, wrongly proportioned furniture to end!

Left: One of my friend Konstantine Kakanias's delightful books; he is a frequent and much-desired houseguest. His books about his alterego, Mrs. Tependris, are hysterical.

Facing: The great room looking towards the dining area and upper mezzanine.

> "Architecture without furniture is not a home. Furniture without curtains is not a room."
>
> — Windsor Smith, interior designer

HARDWARE for various curtains and other window treatments was missing or inadequate and needed to be replenished. After an initial inventory, one thing that was really notable was the incredible diversity of design of the various curtain rods and attaching stanchions: each was a variation of the same simple elements and was uniquely inspired by an invested on-site blacksmith artisan. None of them matched, which I loved. This irregularity gives the house its soul. Normally you would see a single curtain rod design repeated throughout the entire house, as an accomplished design scheme will be arrived upon and then serve as a template for every other rod and stanchion in the house. But not this guy. He was experimenting; he was playing; he was having fun! Mr. Lucking obviously gave his blacksmith an extremely long leash to outfit the estate with designs from his ample imagination.

Uniformity in material makes it possible for non-matching designs to live well together, as in the stanchions that hold the curtain rods in the facing photograph. Their differences celebrate the handcrafted quality of the ironwork. And the space between the curtains is a perfect setting for one of my favorite pieces of furniture—a Sicilian side table naively painted in turquoise and burnt sienna. This piece will always come with me.

LIGHTING FIXTURES in this house had originally been almost exclusively sconces, which provide only an ambient level of lighting that is lovely, but not really adequate. When I look back through the reference material on older Spanish Colonial Revival houses, I am always struck by the overwhelming gloominess of the interiors. Interior darkness in tandem with so much heavy wood reminds me of a somber Vincent Price in *The Fall of the House of Usher* or that oppressive Norma Desmond mansion in *Sunset Boulevard.* Period correctness be damned: the resulting lighting scheme at the ranch, composed of properly placed sconces along with variable floor and table lamps, creates a pleasing and romantic ambience. The quality of the light is warmer and softer and can be better adjusted to enhance and complement the natural sunlight penetrating the windows. And just ask any woman to name one overhead light she considers her ally.

Since it was necessary to rewire the entire house, patch, repair and repaint the interior surfaces anyway, I took all the fixtures off the walls and laid them out in the courtyard. Even with rewiring and a good cleaning, the house still need additional fixtures to meet the basic contemporary standards for interior lighting. I scoured Santa Barbara auction houses and local dealers for appropriate period sconces but it was, in fact, at a flea market in Albi, near my home in southwestern France, that I found the perfect fixtures for the great room. Although originally made for candles, these very heavy, very Spanish Inquisition sconces were beautifully in keeping with the style of the house and would only need to be retrofitted for electric light.

Ironwork

The extraordinary custom ironwork at the Libbey Ranch was something I noticed the minute I entered the property. Everything from light fixtures, chandeliers and staircase railings to window grilles, gate hinges and door straps had been fabricated at the on-site forge by an unknown craftsman of awesome skill and ingenuity. Even the weather vane atop the turret was original to the 1930s construction, fashioned from a stockpile of discarded horseshoes by the on-site blacksmith, Jack Dron. There were fabulous ornamental latches, hinges and knockers that I had not seen anywhere else in the States. The work was unpretentious and is still in excellent condition after decades of use and exposure to the elements. But it was also gorgeously detailed and extremely captivating artistically—clearly Mr. Dron was a craftsman of the highest order.

After a two-decades-long errand searching out adequate vintage hardware with which to outfit various design conceptions of mine, imagine my elation at finding so much inspiration in one place. I had the same feeling (although a completely different style) when I visited Viscaya, the John Deering estate in Florida. In the past I had found it virtually impossible to source old curtain rods, door handles, switch plates, and

> "The décor had that quiet confident quality that emphasized elegant rusticity without overselling it."
>
> —Mel Bourdeaux, writer

such. The sort of ironwork expertise I had been looking for was simply vanishing in the wake of mass production knockoffs at competitive prices. You can still find good hardware in Europe, but, then, the inventory over there has been accumulating for centuries.

While the in situ fixtures at the property were ravishing from a design aesthetic, their implementation was sometimes suspect or obsolete or just plain weird. For example, the wall sconces were routinely placed far too close to windows to make sense and left very little room for ample window treatments to clear. On a first pass, you almost didn't see these mistakes, but the dictates of modern sensibilities called for eventual correction of these earlier oversights.

To supplement the existing ironwork, I haunted the local Ventura County auctions over the course of several months and found pieces from older Spanish Colonial Revival houses in the area. One of the best finds was a set of hand-forged fire tools that was executed at a scale exactly suited for the great room fireplace. They were one of a kind and a perfect match for the design aesthetic I was crafting for the ranch.

AT THE LIBBEY RANCH

there was a variety of well-maintained Talavera tile on-site, which I kept and added to. Authentic period tile really enhances the romance of these Spanish Colonial Revival houses. The glossy, saturated colors of the tiles have delighted the eye in darker rooms for decades, and the subtle discoloration of the original tile work lends further irregularity to these rooms, which were always intended to have a more informal, functional quality than their Gilded Age Mock Tudor counterparts on the North Shore of Chicago.

I love the look and the unpredictability of Talavera tiles, hand painted with the grand colors of Andalucía—rusty reds, cool cobalts, and yawning yellows. In the great room, older-than-the-house Talavera tiles line the risers of the staircase. When I was augmenting the original terra-cotta pavers from the thirties during the kitchen renovation, I inserted a handful of Malibu tiles here and there to break up the flat field of vitrified clay. And before I get completely lost in lust for tile, I need to add that it is resilient, durable and extremely practical.

"Kathryn is blessed with one of those rare eyes
that can pick the best piece at the best price for the best spot.
Furniture mellowed by centuries, faded vintage textiles,
modern art and curious objects all mingle
with gentle insouciance, welcoming you to finally understand
what the French mean by *joie de vivre*."

—Patrick Aumont, owner, Europa antiques, Summerland

After months of making the drive from Santa Monica to Ojai and back via every gallery, antiques shop, and "to the trade" dealer, I simply could not find the perfect work of art to fill the space over the fireplace. I have always been a believer in serendipity, happy accidents and lucky finds; on the other hand, relying on kismet at the eleventh hour is the surest way to blow an unnecessary amount of the budget on a mediocre, uninspired placeholder.

Just before the wrap party, my girlfriend Ursula Brooks dragged me on a treasure hunt through the designer district of Los Angeles in search of the last odds and ends that I needed to really pull the principal rooms together. Ursula, an actress by trade but an antiquarian by nature, had her own network of favorite shops and secret sources. Like me, she moves at the speed of sound. The two of us together waste no time working the rooms of antiques dealers.

Ursula insisted we go into just one more shop, where, leaning against a far wall at the rear, I saw a framed canvas with its back to me. It was the perfect size and scale to fill the fireplace back at the ranch, if its subject matter were anything that I could live with. My exhaustion and elation had worked me into such a euphoric state that I heard myself coughing to the dealer, "I'll take it," before even mustering the energy and inclination to see the thing turned around. To my great surprise, it was a divine portrait of a fetchingly vague young Spanish senorita in profile, from sometime in the late nineteenth century, all black fabric and lace shawl and creamy white skin. Neither "relieved" nor "born again" comes close to describing my emotions lurching out of that shop with that lovely portrait wrapped and tucked under my arm. And the price was right!

Hamish Bowles teaching me how to pose for a *Vogue* shoot.

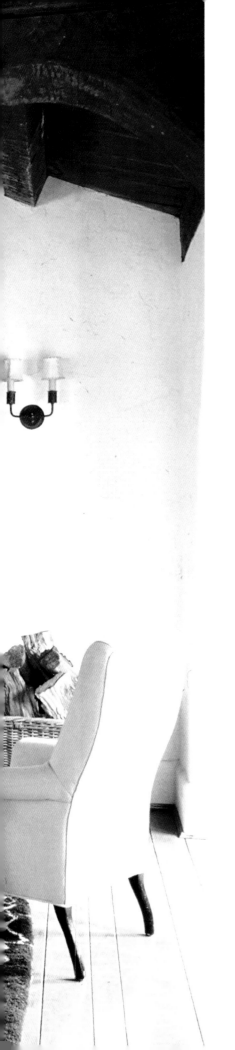

WOOD roughly hewn is one of the three major building elements in all variations of Hispanic and Spanish Colonial Revival residences. Historically, structural grade lumber wasn't easily obtained in the arid Mediterranean region; nor was the situation much different in the analogous climate of Southern California.

In the early twentieth century, a scenario ensued in which timber was hauled down from the foothills of the Sierra and used to reinforce the doorjambs, window casements and corners of ground-floor construction. The strongest lengths of wood stock were used as ceiling beams for roofs tiled with heavy clay and mortar. These rafters and beams were left exposed and, because they typically darkened with age, provided dramatic contrast to the light stucco of the walls and the bright colors of fabric and furnishings. The finest grained and widest planks of old-growth hardwood were reserved for flooring.

To me, character is always more important than perfection. For people and for houses, character is only acquired through life experience. In rooms that are essentially plaster walls and open-beamed ceilings, the only character that is really visible comes from the scratches and scuffs on the floor. The floors are the point of greatest contact any inhabitant will ever have with a house. It's where rugs are rolled up and dancing is done, where old furniture is moved out and new furniture moved in, where babies learn to crawl. Pets, ambient moisture, and all means of uneven care conspire to take a toll on the thickest of old-growth floorboard. Houses settle. So floorboards milled decades ago will shift, expand, and "cup"—creating irregularities I find exceedingly charming and very much removed from the perfectly smooth and even-toned aesthetic of contemporary houses.

NOOKS & CORNERS

Contrary to popular opinion with regard to interior designers, I never feel that a room must be decorated or filled to its very limit with furniture, objects and attention. In fact, I like to leave a variety of spaces on both wall and floor to allow a room to breathe, to grow. My simple rule of thumb, typically, is to place furniture and ornament exactly where I believe it is needed and to benignly neglect the balance of the space.

Paying particular attention to the commonly overlooked square footage in corners, odd alcoves or distant quadrants of any house is a must. Whether these oddments of square footage are large or small, intimate or exposed, convenient or remote, you will do well to attend to the warming and outfitting of these. Spies, of course, love corners so they can scan the room without any obvious craning of the neck, but any civilian alone in a room with more than thirty minutes to spare will seek out and inhabit a well-designed corner. The adjunct to the principal rooms allows one or a couple to quietly gather for conversation or a cocktail or tryst without the momentousness of carrying on in the middle of any room. You might call this "under the radar" or "sotto voce" or "on the down low," but humans do love the small but inestimable sense of security and coziness and predictability found in these forgotten provinces of any residence.

THE BALCONY

at the end of the vaulted great room overlooks the room itself with some lovely wrought iron at waist height. It's an Andalusian balcony really, though I much prefer the romance of referring to it as a "Juliet" balcony. Either way, it is a common feature of the architecture of the Mediterranean, as it allows for a very large opening in an exterior wall where an actual overhanging balcony might not be feasible. It is really invigorating to stand at such a balcony and survey the sea or the hills of Umbria or the Algarve. At the ranch, it is just a lovely little architectural nod to the Old World and a nice purposeful destination for the pleasant meandering of an afternoon.

Once the stable boy's room, this intimate space with its circular walls and French windows opening up to the courtyard provides a cozy reprieve from the grand scale of the great room.

THE Kitchen

Few would argue that the kitchen is absolutely the heart of any house. By the clock, bedrooms may actually contain their inhabitants for more hours and living rooms might be where more unbroken leisure time is spent, but the kitchen is the room everyone in the family knows by heart—the locations of bowls, blenders, silver, corkscrews, nut crackers, flashlights and the hidden chocolate stash.

"Being a native Californian who loves to cook,
I think Ireland's kitchen is perfect! The open shelving
and well-appointed appliances make it light,
airy, and easy to move around—so much so that I was
able to turn out a feast for fifty without a problem!"

— Nathan Turner, antiques dealer

It really doesn't matter how many rooms are available for a party; if you are the hostess and you are doing the cooking, in all likelihood your guests will invade the tightest of quarters to seek you out and be part of the proceedings. Sometimes the most fun and memorable moments are those spent just reliving the day with one's kids or gossiping over the cutting board with a friend or lover. That whole notion of banishing the kitchen, along with the laundry, to the farthest recesses of the house is no longer de rigueur.

Physically rearranging a floor plan to put the kitchen in its most fortuitous location, even if it means yanking everything out, from the plumbing to the countertops, is where I start with a house.

As this is a house that was already clearly about entertaining friends and family, it was not necessary to change the floor plan, but it needed updating to include the necessary appliances to handle a mass of people. A double fridge is imperative. The countertops should be hard wearing, so I used Caesar Stone; it's a lot easier to maintain than limestone, which is gorgeous but too porous and a nightmare to keep up. The food preparation island is really indispensable to a functional and gracious kitchen. It allows for a busy host or hostess to wrap things up, get the menu on the table and still have a look at his or her guests, banter face to face, and not miss a beat. No one wants to talk to anyone's back outside of the bedroom.

Having been a carriage house initially, the existing kitchen was atypically open in plan and very large—a remarkable advantage when working with these older houses. It was almost a replica of the kitchen at my farmhouse in France, which is a conversion of a stable building, similarly large and open.

The agricultural origins of the kitchen did leave it with a very heavy and ubiquitous use of wood, too overpowering for me and in need of some editing. The very dark wood beams running the full length and width of the ceiling created a heavy grid that weighed down the room and closed in what otherwise would have been a light and open space. To reduce this claustrophobic effect, I had the beams running the length of the room painted out with the off-white I was using throughout the house.

With any restoration, preserving the soul of the place is as important to me as the physical structure itself. So many people over-restore and literally scrap away the history and personality, leaving behind a new, sterile interior.

The kitchen needed new cabinetry and appliances. The upper cabinets were removed to make way for open shelving. The existing island that had been made out of an old oversized door needed replacing with a functionally designed piece that the Viking Range could sit in. I like to look out towards another room when cooking rather than at a blank wall. Appliances are important; they're the sine qua non of modern living. It is possible to use contemporary kitchen materials and appliance technology without going completely stainless and clinical and conceding every grace note of warmth in the process.

THE "DRIVE-IN"

fireplace, constructed out of native river rock and stones, is so massive it literally spills out into the kitchen area. It was built in the 1920s by local stone mason Emile Faure for Mr. Lucking, who wanted the round boulders superimposed one on top of the other as though they were "a pile of balls." As you can see from the historic photo to the left, Lucking's fireplace enclosure was of sufficient dimension to shelter an alcove dining area. And, as there was no central heating and the average low temperature in the Ojai Valley during the winter months dips to 35 degrees, having a fireplace that beckons one inside makes perfect sense.

My updated arrangement of furniture repositioned a larger dining table closer to the kitchen end of the room, thereby creating a full sitting area, complete with deep, wide sofa and two swivel chairs in front of Lucking's magnificent "pile of balls." I converted a large Indian door into a coffee table and situated colorful ottomans directly on the hearth, for those of us who can never be too warm.

Left: Grouping various objects is a simple and effective way to decorate. Nothing should ever seem too important or outshine anything else. I like objects to live side by side harmoniously.

Right: This catchall, found at Big Daddy's stand at the Santa Monica Flea Market, is a useful must-have for any kitchen. It holds pans above, shelters liquor beneath and is a place to lay your handbag.

THE FLOOR TILES in the kitchen are vintage Mexican pavers and are original to the house, having been laid in a Versailles pattern, following architect Austen Pierpont's direction at the time of the conversion from barn to residence in the early 1930s. During my renovation, it was necessary to both replace broken tile and augment freshly liberated areas of flooring with newer pieces that were visibly "younger" than their mates in shade and finish. These sorts of imperfections I can live with. In fact, I secretly hope that they will arise in the course of any renovation as I think they are the final accent to a successful installation, like the last-minute artful dishevelment by a woman just before leaving the house to avoid looking "too done." As for the inconsistencies with the tile, I simply tossed a few Moroccan rugs, colorful and durable, across the tricky areas. But I would have done that anyway, to create the layered, lived-in look that is my signature.

The examples on the right are variations on the pavers that are available today. Mixing up the different shapes for different rooms is quirky and less uniform. Using the same color and material is enough continuity for me. Houses should look like they have evolved over the years, something that's hard to achieve with a spec house.

"She came looking for a big bowl to put on a table in the great room, but she left wearing cowboy chaps, a hat and a whip."

— Ilon Specht
owner of Hacienda, Ojai

POTTERY is great for accent pieces. Part of the fun of bringing a large-scale residential restoration to a close and something that I look forward to is the search for those great accent pieces—paintings, pottery, worked wood, random objets d'art—that will punch up the interiors and enliven the dialogue between the furniture and the rooms themselves. Objects create a first impression, appealing or not, so I try to ferret out pieces that not only catch my eye but also relate in some organic way to the balance of my design effort. I like to marry the traditions of similar but geographically distinct regions, or to pair furniture with objects that share similar lines or shapes or hues yet derive from antagonistic traditions or cultures. It's really effective to place modern or contemporary pieces into a graciously preserved period home: the only criterion I need is that some story, history or scholarship connects the juxtaposition, something beyond simple prettiness.

Local dealers and flea markets are the best places to look for such artifacts. The Ojai Valley has a long and very robust history of bohemians, ex-patriots, artists, hippies and even well-heeled rustics who patronized local artists and acquired furnishings that were relevant to the emerging aesthetic. Consequently, there is a substantial body of fantastic pieces and potential finds circulating through the community and an experienced cadre of dealers locating new and equally worthy pieces to augment existing stock.

One of my favorite discoveries in Ojai is a small shop called Hacienda. Its owner, Ms. Ilon Specht, has collected a remarkable inventory of Mexican pottery and wooden furnishings, painted artwork in various media, and primitive handcrafted metalwork. The instant I stepped through the door, I was immediately salivating at her extraordinary selection of Oaxacan dripware (vintage Mexican tourist pottery) as well as old *santos* and other religious relics. I was easily sold on an enormous amount of very collectible early to mid-twentieth-century Mexican pottery—pieces from Tlaquepaque, a little artists' enclave outside of Guadalajara famous for the quality of its clay, and also from the impossibly spelled pre-Columbian artisan's village of Tzintzuntzan, in the state of Michoacan. New pottery in these same traditions continues to be produced, so I decided on a jumble of vintage and contemporary pieces. Ilon was exceedingly helpful with the very arduous selection process, providing history and background on the colors and motifs used on the pieces, on traditional function and customary pairing. She also knew how to locate those types and sizes of pottery that I had envisioned for specific areas at the Ojai property but that she didn't have in her shop.

A dresser is so much more attractive than endless built-ins. I like kitchens to be rooms that have their own character. The combination of texture, material and color bring a room to life.

Thrilled with all of the pottery and other objects I sourced at Hacienda, I am still most taken with the green-and-white dripware that is so vivid and evocative and makes for great contrast with the neutral tones on the walls and floors of the residence. These pieces are not just eminently decorative and still useful, but they add another layer to the "lamination" process I employ in my interior design work.

The crockery that is on display is a hodgepodge of old French storage canisters, Mexican pottery, Italian glassware and decorative Spanish majolica.

Doors and Doorknobs

As carefree and nonchalant as I have become about home security in the French countryside, fully operational doors and windows and locks are not anything to disregard in even the most placid districts of Southern California. Many of the interior doors at the Libbey Ranch featured their original hardware dating from the early '30s, around the time of the conversion of outbuildings into additional living quarters. In fact, these original doors with their patinated black hardware compose one of the most uniform and striking accents throughout the house. All of these doorknobs, hinges, latches and locksets were made by the resident black-

smith at the forge on the far side of the property. Indeed, throwing over the large bolt to the massive front door was like locking up some remote castle in Scotland. There was nothing flimsy or expedient about any of this hardware. The simple shapes were emphatically rustic, masculine, solid and reassuring. I refabricated missing components and augmented them where newer standards of home security dictated, but essentially these doorknobs and locksets remain very much intact—as beautiful and functional and rare as they likely were at their outset, though they no doubt get more use in our more private age.

Left: The inherent beauty and value of anything handmade lies in its irregularity and imperfection—its uniqueness. All of the original artisanal door hardware further enhanced the already considerable charm and authenticity of the property. **Facing:** The actual door to this doorway is long gone, so I chose to hang a curtain (made out of Italian linen from my woven line) on an old wrought-iron curtain rod that I had discovered junked in a remote corner of the carriage house. The chaps hanging from the coat rack in the entry area were a crazy impulse buy at Hacienda that worked perfectly here.

Above: Copious use of texturing techniques and revealed hammer marks are really well articulated and eye-catching when executed in wrought iron.
Right: These simple cupboard doorknobs with a Moorish flourish seem almost dainty compared to the heavy, sculptural look and feel that characterizes the majority of iron hardware at the Libbey Ranch.

Though various and idiosyncratic, the door hardware was consistent in one respect: all of it exhibited the same sort of finely crude, hand-made, one-of-a-kind aesthetic. These pieces reveal the inherent beauty of the iron and the craftsmanship with which it was worked.

THE Bedrooms & Bathrooms

After fifteen-plus years at my Santa Monica home, my own bedroom, the master suite, is still the hub of all the life upstairs. It's where everyone congregates, family obviously, as well as new and old friends. It's where many staff meetings take place, where my kids and their friends sprawl out on my bed and watch their football games and bootlegged DVDs, where my closest girlfriends come to gossip and console and, surprisingly, where my male friends tell me their secrets.

I found, somewhat to my surprise, that I actually loved
the solitude available in each of the bedrooms.
But the master suite, more remote than the others,
afforded a complete sort of seclusion.

The layout at the ranch, however, was such that the various bedrooms are only accessible from the outside. These bedrooms are actually true sanctuaries of privacy and retreat, wanted or not. Somewhat to my surprise, I actually loved the solitude available in each of the bedrooms. But the master suite, more remote than the others, afforded a complete sort of seclusion. Its location made it ineligible for casual dropping in, an unlikely destination for any but the most urgent or amorous of missions. No one would venture there unless they had a very good reason. Naturally, I could still hear my kids and their friends in the adjoining rooms as need be, but otherwise this master suite with its solid option for privacy had a real weekend away/holiday feel to it.

Before the renovation, the master suite also had an interesting, somewhat unwieldy warren of rooms opening off of it—a walk-in closet and a dressing area appointed with a sink but lacking the lav or shower. The first order of business, then, was to rearrange this square footage, to install a proper bathroom and re-outfit a useful and roomy closet. Although we accomplished all of this successfully, there were some impediments that are amusingly recollected over cocktails but which my brother Robert will still cringe over. We spent days digging into the granite-addled dirt to get all of the new pipe laid.

What constitutes a successful master suite? A handful of elements that are indispensable, in no particular order of importance: a very good king-sized mattress set, a wood-burning fireplace, some kind of awning over the bed or swagged, tented fabric, a signature color, a lovely view and a bookcase filled with one's favorite books. It is the stone-clad fireplace that made this room.

The room is also blessed with good natural light. I added forest green jacquard linen curtains from my collection as minimal window treatments and hung them with one pleat on simple iron rings. This allowed the light to penetrate the room easily in the mornings.

As relates to the selected furnishings for this room, I kept the design scheme completely simple. Cricket tables became bedside table holding simple lamps that I dressed up using random oddments of leftover Robert Kime fabric. An astute but nevertheless terribly true observation is that, like pillows, lampshades require only a very little amount of yardage to execute but contribute a disproportionate amount of punch to the space. They are my reliable quick fixes—affordable and remarkably useful as accents. The room had many charming nooks for books and photos and various found objects. I dressed up the bed set with a tailored bedskirt and various coverlets.

THE MASTER bedroom renovation at the ranch was involved and lengthy. I really did find myself living and working in each one of the twenty-odd rooms, something quite atypical for an interior designer. One fantastic upshot to this nomadic stint was that I became intimately acquainted with the qualities of each room prior to any principal design work. I knew when and where the morning light fell. I knew where it might be comfortable to read and where the logical choice was for placing a bed.

Of particular interest to me were the various views from each of these rooms. Since much planting had occurred over the last century, there was a fair amount of vegetation to work with. There were the coast live oaks that were ancient and untouchable fixtures around which to anchor the rest of the work. And there were vines—wisteria, bougainvillea, morning glory, and English ivy—and eucalyptus and more eucalyptus, lovely, messy and fast growing. Art directing the view really amounted to taming and shaping the eucalyptus, which was a unifying note around the property.

A few days into my tenure in the master bedroom, I knew that the existing windows were simply not adequate to capture the spectacular vista that was just outside those walls. The dense blue-green foliage of eucalyptus was lovely, but there was a whole meadow outside waiting to be seen and a dramatic ridge of the Topa Topa Mountains that would light up brightly at dawn.

I instinctively enlarged the window to the right of the fireplace so that this entire tableau of Southern California chaparral was visible from the bed and elsewhere around the room. Even with the new and improved window, I was still not convinced that every picturesque inch had been claimed from this view. More pruning and thinning would give me the wide-screen, VistaVision, Jumbotron panorama I craved. One morning I invited my gardener into my bedroom and insisted that he lie down on the bed with me in order to appreciate the view—or almost view. It was infinitely easier to show him what I wanted than to articulate my desires. And he instantly knew which trees had to go. In about an hour's time I had what I wanted, or at least the view I had been banging on about.

Fireplaces

After decamping Great Britain in my twenties, I have lived almost every day since in temperate Mediterranean-like climates—mostly dry, with typically warm and sunny days and temperatures that drop quickly after dusk. These patterns are true much of the year in coastal California, in the southwest of France, in Morocco and on the west coast of Mexico. And I am an enthusiastic convert to the lifestyle this climate engenders—cottons and linens and bare skin during the day, light wool wraps and long skirts and wood fires after dark.

Conventional wisdom decries the lack of seasons in California, but there is daily seasonality to life along the Pacific. Twenty-degree temperature swings from the misty June-gloom mornings to desert-hot afternoons and back to half-chilly sunsets are dramatic in their own ways. In any event, fireplaces have always been integral to life in these climates, and I consider them to be indispensable.

Fireplaces are at once compelling décor and practical necessities. There has never been any shortage of granite fieldstone, river rock or beach stone with which to build in Southern California, and so a tradition of more irregular and informal fireplaces ensued, gaining popularity alongside the early Arts and Crafts movement and bungalow craze. The surviving fireplaces in many Southern California homes are really remarkably sculptural, sinuous and organic and paler than the red brick or limestone fireplaces of eastern American or European homes.

The temperature fluctuation in the Ojai Valley is very much like I have described, with marked nighttime temperature drops from Halloween through Easter. Not surprisingly, the rambling structures at the Libbey Ranch featured a grand total of eight wood-burning fireplaces, ranging in size from the massive ski lodge edition in the kitchen to the small adobe kiva fireplaces tucked into many of the bedroom corners. Whether crackling and fully ablaze or simply at the ready with a handy stack of eucalyptus and piñon pine, a fireplace is the de facto architectural focal point of a room. What I love about the fireplaces in this house is that their proportions are just exquisite, perfectly sized in every room. Even the diminutive kivas in the bedrooms really look and feel integral and essential. And in the larger, more public, rooms the scale and elaboration of the fireplaces are just beautiful.

Obviously, we have some environmental responsibilities related to wood-burning fires today. Decades ago in this valley, building a fire around sunset was a daily ritual, as was the gathering and stacking of the wood. There was ample fuel to be had in the downed limbs of sycamores, cottonwoods, coast live oaks, fast-growing California laurel and various rangy pines. Starting and tending to fires was something of an art, and the smell of woodsmoke is a sensory pleasure that clean and efficient natural gas cannot match. Now we have fires you can turn on with keys. But making a fire, keeping it going, and then watching it die out as you go to bed is a ritual worth preserving.

The painting above the fireplace is by my childhood friend India Jane Birley, the talented granddaughter of the twentieth-century society portrait painter Sir Oswald Birley.

"Kathryn works with color in the same way that an artist works with paint . . .
she layers color upon color to achieve her signature palette.
It changes with each interior, yet continues to be innovative and
exciting . . . as well as particularly expressive for each client."

—Judi Roaman, owner, J. Roaman, East Hampton

The guest suite proved to be an unexpected challenge during the renovation. What had once been stables, then converted into a workshop, was now not more than a shell. With an iconoclastic mixture of furnishings, vibrant fabrics, and highly contrasting, straightforward white stucco walls, this guest room became so popular with returning friends and family that it was frequently fought over!

The combination of Oberto Gigli's contemporary photograph, the eighteenth-century English four-poster bed and the mixture of colorful textiles in this room make a great marriage. The bed sits on a Moroccan berber rug of creams and browns that adds a calmness to this sea of color. This is a perfect example of how different periods and styles can happily live side by side.

IN SELECTING PAINTS for interior walls, I went with my natural inclination toward paler shades of primary colors or basic neutrals, as I invariably rely upon the layering of textiles and fabrics to add color and interest. For the interiors here, I re-created the neutral off-white background shade of the natural hemp that I use to print my fabric designs by mixing Farrow and Ball "Clunch" and Benjamin Moore "Timid White."

Interior doors, trim and moldings needed to be defined so as to punctuate and provide scale to the room—a color contrast that makes accent woodwork pop. I wanted to use a color reminiscent of the ubiquitous blue-green shutters one sees along the Adriatic, Aegean, and Amalfi coasts, and was able to communicate this visual sense memory to Reuven, my painter of many years. He concocted several shades from a simple white base and straightforward universal tints that attempted to conjure this remote maritime geography.

"The various hues and textures of decorative tile add romance and intrigue to any historical or contemporary setting."

— Jodi Pecka, Creative Director, Malibu Ceramic Works

Tile

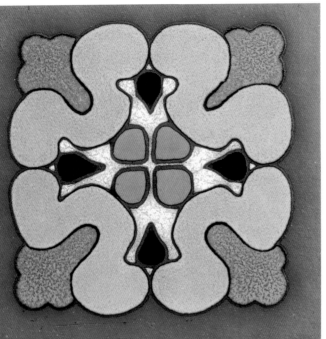

Prior to attaining current status as a visual cue card for gracious indoor/outdoor California living, brightly colored decorative tile work that is now synonymous with every variation on Hispanic and Mediterranean architecture from Bel Air to Bolinas has had a long and noble heritage. In the Spanish Colonial Revival period, tile found fantastic application on risers of sculptural staircases, as visual relief across expanses of terra-cotta floor pavers and white stucco walls as blank as stretched canvases, as accents about fireplace surrounds, as integral elements in kitchens and baths, and as artful components to niches and follies anywhere the architect found himself with an odd corner or barren passage. The use of tile introduced the palette of the Mediterranean into these otherwise neutral rooms, creating concentrated jewel-like punctuations that are at once elegant and playful.

Tiles on the left are modern-day reproductions that bring a sense of history and place, like being somewhere in Mexico or Spain.

GUEST COTTAGES

on the estate were located close enough to the main residence so as to not induce any sensation of Siberian exile but remote enough to still afford an ample sense of privacy and discretion. Although modest in size, they both opened up onto the sweeping lawn of the newly configured swimming pool area and Buddha garden. These cozy, intimate cottages were unassumingly constructed and absent of ornament and flourish, so it really didn't take much to bring these unadorned spaces to renewed life. To me, a successful guest room is one that functions like a hotel suite—a clean, neutral space with a good mattress, good pillows, and empty closets and dresser drawers. As there were no built-in closets, I substituted small painted vintage armoires from Hungary that were perfect in size and character. One small chair for catching clothes, extra blankets at the foot of the bed, and good bedside lamps are essential. They don't have to match, especially in a cottage, although I think having pairs of something is good for the balance of the room. Here I have a pair of English pine bedside tables. This allows the room to be visually organized without being too done while at the same time not looking like a "jumble sale." Keeping guest rooms as spare and simple as possible gives my guests "a length of leash" to personalize a room with their own possessions and feel that much more comfortable during their stay.

BATHROOMS

Bathrooms in older homes usually require work during any renovation, whether "sympathetic" or not—most likely a fair amount of plumbing upgrade. You won't know exactly what this work will entail until you start looking behind walls and within crawl spaces, but guaranteed there is wear, failure, or deferred maintenance somewhere.

Repairs of this sort are relatively straightforward and absolutely necessary, as is any replacement of imperfect though unseen copper plumbing throughout the residence. Trickier aesthetic decisions, which may have significant impact on any construction budget, involve the degree to which period porcelain fixtures and nickel or pewter faucet sets are removed and reconditioned or simply replaced. Though I truly loved the classic shapes of the existing washstands and bathtubs, and they were exactly what I would have chosen, their condition would have necessitated an enormous amount of costly repair and refinishing plus replating of the metal and some creative plumbing to reinstall them. It ultimately turned out to be less time consuming and more cost effective to simply replace the original porcelain with a selection of quality contemporary reproductions that are readily available.

"Creating a 'lived-in' house that makes people feel good and
relaxed isn't easy. A lot of effort goes into
striking a balance of simplicity, function, and visual harmony."

—Louise Fletcher, actress

Above: I purchased this sweet painted chair from the previous owner. This basic side
table with a few drawers provides storage for extra towels and bathroom essentials.
The oil painting is from Louise Fletcher's collection of nineteenth- and twentieth-century art
that I've been acquiring for years. The colorful bath mat on the floor is actually
a horse blanket from Argentina. **Facing:** A good-sized tub is essential for any bathroom.

The small adobe fireplaces, kivas actually, in the bathrooms and the bedrooms were the only real heat sources for early inhabitants of the ranch.

When I gutted the guest cottages, fortunately I was able to locate excellent period-inspired tub and faucet hardware that was perfectly in keeping with the dominant aesthetic. Really spectacular hardware is always worth the effort to recondition; the same is true for very large or uniquely shaped footed tubs. But there is a fair amount of ambiguousness with regard to pieces of slightly lesser appeal. Let the market and your own eye be your guide. There is a much greater selection available today than there was even a decade ago, so you can assume that what you are looking for is likely to be available.

TILE AND GROUT.

The words and the work are not pretty. Grouting is a messy, many-part process that is taken for granted. The color, density, consistency, width and seal are all nearly as important as the sizing, color, and pattern of the tiles themselves. Wider grout lines are popular because they speed up the work of the tile setter and reduce the materials cost by using fewer tiles, but this is a foolish place to economize.

In very small doses, heavy, wide grouting seams can be architectural and bold, but they can very quickly overpower an entire bath or kitchen. Dove or oyster gray hues contrast just enough with the ruddy tones of terracotta to enliven the work. Bones and beiges are always elegant. If in doubt, go light. This is not the place to get experimental.

Left: The existing floor plan had the other bedrooms quite modest in size, so I wanted to create one guest suite for conventional needs and tastes. Since I had the luxury of carving up raw open space in the converted stable block, I was able to make this bathroom contemporary and capacious. **Right:** Like lampshades and pillows, drawer pulls are a fun and inexpensive way to simultaneously refresh old furnishings and dab a room with small strokes of color or shine that will not overwhelm. Cut crystal, brushed metal, or painted ceramic knobs can imbue otherwise standard equipment with personality.

Al Fresco Living

In the 1930s, the Libbey property had been designed with courtyard, terraces, and verandas for entertaining and leisure. Today the unquestionably picturesque living quarters, barns, outbuildings, and spaces in between all continue to lend themselves to a great variety of impromptu meals, cocktail efforts, boisterous conversations or simple hanging out, alone or with one's tribe. While these spaces were all allowed for and adequately designed, their actual execution and inherent efficiency were not exactly what they could have been—certainly not when considering the lives of early-twenty-first-century families like my own.

THE FORECOURT and façade, encompassing the turret, graceful staircase and second-floor balcony, are what I initially fell in love with. The actual court itself was a hodgepodge of uneven flagstone, portions of lawn and random plantings. We cleaned and pruned the space and then planted lavender, rosemary and roses.

The flagstone I had used throughout the estate seemed too hard and permanent for this garden-like environment, so I decided to spill the pea gravel from the driveway into a sweep around the courtyard. Advice I was once given by a neighbor in France was that gravel deters robbers because of the crunching sound it makes underfoot. Robbers never worried me, but I had already surrounded my farm-house with gravel to keep tabs on any of my horses that may have broken out of their fields in the middle of the night. In creating a home, the focus for me is to effortlessly integrate the indoors and outdoors, allowing the laughter of friends, squealing delight of children, barking of dogs and neighing of horses to become the background music.

In this way I was able to preserve the spirits of both Libbey and Lucking.

The centerpiece of the U-shaped structure designed by Wallace Neff for Libbey was a circular tower that connected the wings for cow milking and carriage stalls.

The splashing delight of this water element immediately became the charmer, the piper; and with the morning sun as its accomplice, it continues to draw the sensualists out of the house for breakfast and coffee.

The newly transformed courtyard cried out for more focus, a little visual interest positioned right in the center. The old tree that originally stood here was past its "sell-by" date. I stumbled upon a large Spanish earthenware pot that I had fitted out as a fountain and built another fieldstone base upon which to showcase this new treasure. The splashing delight of this water element immediately became the charmer, the piper; and with the morning sun as its accomplice, it continues to draw the sensualists out of the house for breakfast and coffee. Easy access to this charmingly renovated forecourt is now possible via French doors from all sides—from the newly configured master bedroom (formerly a stable), the kitchen and the great room. Remarkably, the renovation of the forecourt instantly enlarged and made more attractive each of these surrounding rooms, adding a romantic opportunity even if only glimpsed through the glass of a door on a rainy day.

Strange, delicately pointed arches frame the front portal. Although Libbey died before he could realize his complete vision for a working ranch estate, the cat and dog carved on the gate entrance to the forecourt literally illustrate the childlike delight this powerful man was investing in his creation, along with his belief that utility and beauty go hand in hand. The gates have been scrupulously cherished and maintained by various owners for decades. Pushing through these doors is like entering the magical realm of "the weekend." Animal carvings, not an easily accomplished folk art, decorate all of the gates and are a signature note of the ranch.

Facing: The former gardener's shed now houses the newly centralized mechanical and electrical systems for the estate.
Right: The whimsical cutouts on the gates date back to Libbey's day. Wallace Neff had incorporated these cutouts into the original barn design. We loved them so much that we commissioned additional carvings to extend the motif elsewhere on the estate. This rooster perches on a new gate leading to the pool area.

Adobe

Rare as actual adobe is in this day and age, I have had experience with this most quixotic and temperamental of building materials. Many of the French renovations I have overseen were of simple nineteenth-century rural or even agricultural structures that had made use of this very crude but abundant building technology. The oldest houses in Southern California necessarily incorporated adobe in their construction, and many of these still remain in the more rarified districts of the Southland, where their authentic charm is much sought after. The composition and application of adobe bricks does vary with region, topography, and climate, but it is uniformly low tech—some mixture of clay and sand with straw, horsehair, broken pottery, ash, or even farm animal dung. Old adobe can be strong and lasting,

provided it has somehow remained protected from moisture encroachment and pest infestation. The most important consideration when working with this material is that it be carefully and appropriately sealed with plaster, stucco or whitewash and that it be monitored and maintained with some degree of vigilance. It is truly an evocative and unique construction technique and entirely worthy of renovation, but it does present considerably more challenge than wood frame or even other forms of masonry construction.

The solidity and horizontality of structures built of adobe really provide the sine qua non of recognizable Spanish Colonial or Mission Revival architecture, although the rambling heavy red clay tile roofs are also integral to this rustic and picturesque presentation. Interestingly,

very little about the look of these adobe structures relates to aesthetics. The long and low massing of the structure was due to the nature of the load-bearing capacity of adobe blocks, which is considerably less than that of brick or stone. To support the same structural loads, adobe is typically two or three times the thickness of these other more familiar materials, and, thus, adobe structures appear much larger and thicker and have fewer doors and windows in their facades. Owing to the wall thickness and infrequent and very recessed fenestration, the interior spaces are very quiet and somewhat dark due to lack of direct sunlight. Well insulated, adobe interiors are also naturally cool and sharply shadowed, a relief from the cloudless sunshine and dusty winds that they are frequently subjected to.

Having the recessed windows cut into two- or three-foot exterior walls not only mitigates the harsh exterior light but also provides much additional built-in surface area that is brightly tiled for any use at all—drying or warming or the growing of herbs. These many tiled window ledges set with various pretty things have become a visual hallmark of this architectural style; yet their iconic quality is born out of simple necessity. So much of the Spanish Colonial Revival idiom was dictated by the limitations of the building materials at hand.

The adobe walls at the Libbey Ranch were at least two feet thick and were very simple and unremediated, just raw adobe that had been many times painted over. Not surprisingly, everywhere we found that the wasps and bats had drilled holes into and built nests within the familiar mud of these walls. I set about a restoration that would provide the structural integrity we required while preserving the aesthetic resulting from the age and use of these adobe walls. In the end, we removed the wasps and patched the walls with a very dense though lightweight concrete plaster, repainted the entire lengths of the walls with a thicker coating of sealing white paint.

About halfway through the renovation it became clear that more rewiring was ultimately called for than I had initially been led to believe and that this rewiring was going to need to snake behind these very same restored adobe walls, which were not entirely conducive to being "chased." Electrified wall sconces really offer no alternative to concealed wiring, and the furrowing of wires into old adobe was not going to be easy or quick. Exposed metal conduit running up an exterior wall was a solution I ended up using in guest cottages. We ultimately endeavored to chase out the walls by hand with hammer and chisel and bury the conduit within the interior adobe wall, re-re-plastering over our tracks. This detour was not cheap, but the result is simple and remarkable and more period appropriate. In days of old the sconces held candles; today they hold elegant electric fixtures with parchment shades, and it was worth the additional headache.

Above: The original gatekeeper's cottage is now a small bedroom with sleeping loft. When one wants a less communal experience than the main house is offering, this place is the perfect getaway. **Right:** To make use of this lovely corner of the estate, we cleared some underbrush, retained the sculptural cacti, and made the area more accessible and inviting by creating paths lined with found stone. A daybed underneath this stand of ancient live oaks is a perfect place to escape the heat.

The Herculean task of returning the grounds to their former splendor evolved into a labor of love, as there was so much delightful planting to work with. To have the grandeur of very old specimen oaks and fifty-plus-year-old stands of mature eucalyptus was a true stroke of good fortune. But we still needed to orchestrate a comprehensive overhaul of the grounds, from replacement of the antiquated irrigation systems to the trimming and renovation of various flowering shrubs to the judicious eradication of much of the cacti. Most of the brush, and certainly all of the fallen eucalyptus bark, was a fire hazard and had to be removed. What remained was a classic complement of mature plantings from the original estate, now properly scaled to the larger buildings and providing year-round visual interest.

"The property had a wonderful rustic Scottish castle feel to it. Incredible wrought iron. Wonderful gates and hinge straps. All the latches. Lots of whimsies and wonderful stuff! Whoever did it was into it and enjoyed it. It was obviously something someone loved!"

— Siegfried Wessberg, blacksmith artist

THE FORGE and blacksmith shop at the Libbey Ranch was original to the property from the very beginning. Situated near the old coach house, the shop was well equipped with smithing tools, an anvil and bellows. Rumor has it that all of the intricate ironwork was designed and made right on the property. I've worked with my blacksmith friend Siegfried Wessberg throughout my career, and when I showed him this charming building (you can still see where the forge and fires were) he was bowled over. He understood immediately that the day-to-day demands upon an on-site blacksmith in Libbey's day would have far exceeded the duties of a standard farrier; he would have had to repair and craft tools, sharpen various blades, and fabricate replacement pieces for any of the machines on the property. Simple bolts and screws and fasteners that are now quite easily obtained and cheap were expensive back then and time consuming if made to order. This local blacksmith would likely have even made his own nailheads.

My hope was that in some organic way Siegfried could approximate patina on the new iron fixtures, because I'm allergic to anything forcefully "distressed." He warned me that effecting primitiveness and rusticity would be considerably more expensive than ordering from an online catalog. I have come to really trust my eye and sense of proportion with regard to design budgets and knew I would never regret splurging on custom ironwork. I told Siegfried to put his head down and go where his instincts led him.

THE BREEZEWAY of the house makes great use of that Mediterranean innovation, the outdoor hallway. Having grown up on the windswept shores of Scotland and in the drizzle of London, I am intimately familiar with the necessity of the central hall floor plan—conserving precious heat and minimizing various transit times. But when nature shines on certain climates, why not take advantage and unfold the family home, flinging bedrooms out wide and splaying public rooms around the site to take best advantage of the midday sun and afternoon light?

Previous owners here must have grown weary of this relentless indoor/outdoor living, as they had completely enclosed the breezeway with plate glass and sliding glass doors, very à la mode in the Southern California of the 1970s. Not only was the steel and plate glass incongruous with the balance of the construction, but it was also ill-conceived and unintended irony, sealing hermetically and making stiflingly hot and stuffy that which had been perfectly designed to be cool and breezy. In any event, all of that glass is long gone and I think the residence flows, practically and figuratively, much more organically from room to room.

Stone

Stone is abundant in Southern California. It's a rocky sort of place, with stones and pebbles and boulders and scree everywhere, underneath the lushest of lawns, behind the showiest of bougainvillea. It is a given that gardeners, landscape architects and general contractors will have to devise all manner of scenarios to work around the unseen onslaught of rock. Prius-sized boulders are all over the landscape, and what appears at first glance as soil is actually an uneven mix of decomposing granite, other stone and a much smaller component of humus or decaying vegetation. Canyons, barrancas, ravines, all lined with calved and rolled stones, are everywhere in Ventura and Santa Barbara counties, and the Libbey Ranch in Ojai is largely characterized by this rocky desertlike topography. Part of the reason that so few homes in Southern California have basements is that the excavation costs for the simplest version would be almost prohibitively steep; even the construction of the smallest kidney-shaped pool invariably requires an amount of honest-to-goodness blasting to make headway. My understanding of these matters was gleaned largely through a baptism by fire ensuing from the septic system failure literally contemporaneous with the closing of escrow.

Repair of the septic system, its flow lines and leach fields proved to be a gargantuan undertaking. Throughout trenching we ran into subterranean boulders at every turn, the price tag rising by the square foot. I am not one to re-sling adages around, but in this instance that old "if life throws you lemons . . ." cliché really struck home. Hauling all of the excavated stone off-site would have been outrageously expensive—county waste disposal facilities tend to charge by weight, as if natural California granite were just so much jackhammered concrete. Honestly, you can easily recycle and/or dispose of virtually any other material much more conveniently and inexpensively than hauling untold tons of real rock away. My own version of Ojai lemonade was to aesthetically arrange the largest of the boulders around the estate, building retention walls and laying some surface paving. We further cleaned many of the seasonal watercourses on the property and lined them sporadically with more excavated rock. The upside of all of this repurposing is that the whole property, from boulders left in situ to architecturally utilized shaped granite to landscape features to the punctuation along new and improved creek beds, looks unified and organic and homegrown. And it is.

As it turns out, architects and builders in Southern California have long used this same modus operandi with

regard to the inconvenient truths of rock and stone. These impediments were put to good use in foundations and some walling and bridging, as fieldstone has been utilized for thousands of years. Many of the oldest load-bearing walls around the ranch were constructed of indigenous rock, and their durability and natural beauty continue to this day. As the living quarters were further modernized, more than a few of these exterior stone walls became an exposed section of masonry wall, creating an unpretentious look. No effort was made to plaster over the nicely laid courses of rock in an effort to conceal the growing pains of the structure. Similarly, the many stone fireplaces were left in an unadulterated state, still fully revealing the craftsmanship and aesthetic acumen pulled together decades ago.

Found rock was also handsomely used around doorjambs, as lintels over windows, and as hearths and flooring. All of this familiar and similar rock and stone really does unify the look and feel of this property and lends a particular charm to the meandering walls that still ring the perimeter of the estate surrounding the pool and pool house.

Left: We drained and removed a duck pond that was now a breeding ground for mosquitoes behind the master suite, filled it with excavated rock and soil and installed an appropriately water-conscious lawn where it would be most accessible to and visible from the main residence. **Above:** A small footbridge fashioned out of native rock spans a seasonal creek that cuts across the front lawn. I made use of the extra fieldstone I was constantly digging up in the course of the restoration to further line the watercourses that meandered around the property.

Left: The idea of leaving the main house in order to head off to bed appeals to me; to make a departure with the supplies needed and ritualize the interlude between the day and the night. My brother Robert and his landscaping team created this flagstone path from the main house to the bedroom wing so that evening excursions would be less dicey.
Right: We crisscrossed the property with bridle paths that also serve as walking trails and contoured them with the ubiquitous fieldstone.

Left: The sun playing in ever-changing patterns through the great wide-spreading oaks is the perfect expression of the picturesque and beautiful—and an ideal location for an afternoon nap on daybeds I found in France. **Above** This Buddha, which I left behind and bequeathed to the next chatelaine, further lends a sense of peace and tranquility to the already serene landscape.

"What was once an overgrown lot of brambles and brush transforms into a serene expression of meditative calm, as it was ages ago with the Chumash."

Ian Scott, design consultant

HALF-TIMBERING is an exterior ornamentation derived from medieval construction that left structural timbers exposed and filled the spaces between them with plaster, stone or other material at hand. A popular architectural technique of the Tudor Dynasty, from the 1880s and onward, half-timbering became a visual hallmark of Tudorbethan, or Mock Tudor, and was used to decoratively mimic the appearance of the earlier load-bearing heavy timbers.

Mr. Lucking had fallen in love with the look while traveling in France, or perhaps the Benelux countries, and directed his California architect to incorporate some of the decorative false half-timbering into the emerging architectural melange then taking shape at Ojai.

I chose to paint over the dark brown half-timbering with an accent color I had discovered while paint-scraping some exterior trimwork. One of the earliest colors I found was a soothing shade of blue-green. At various points over the last eighty years, almost all of the trim on the buildings had worn this shade of green proudly.

Today the half-timbering that you see is purely decorative, a finishing cladding with no pure structural effect. It is still quite picturesque and enlivens a length of plaster or stucco wall in an organic and rather nostalgic way.

"The restoration wasn't so much a project as a full on love affair. And it shows. The property has that rare quality: a real living atmosphere as well as perfect pitch between the design choices and the raw bones of the wonderful relic that initially caught her eye."

— Martyn Lawrence-Bullard, interior designer

In his design for the stables on the ranch, Austen Pierpont realized the successful adaptation of an architectural scheme to the environment. The buildings were perfectly harmonized with their surroundings and looked as though they had grown up with the oaks. From the stables, you can ride out into the surrounding mountains on existing horse trails and disappear for days. There are 60,000 acres of state wilderness between Ojai and Santa Ynez, making the area even more extraordinary considering its proximity to the city of Los Angeles.

Above: The bifold wood door opens to the tractor shed, which serves as a combination summer kitchen and storage area for pool equipment. Mexican pavers were laid on bare ground to create a serviceable floor for a functioning kitchen. A window overlooks the barbecue area and allows whoever's cooking to pass things through.
Right: To make room for the swimming pool, we had to cut down several eucalyptus trees. Logs from those trees now fuel the many fireplaces. Nothing goes to waste.
Facing: Instead of repainting them, I left some of the gates and doors that were stained dark brown alone, primarily because I didn't want all the woodwork on the ranch to be matchy-matchy Ojai Green, as I now call it.

Entertaining

I'm a great believer in creating an assortment of outdoor spaces that can function as rooms, so I was thrilled that the property came with stunning and unimaginably photogenic areas for entertaining. Unfortunately, not all were practical. My original idea to create a charming outdoor dining room under the branches of a hillside coast live oak was abandoned when I realized what a chore it would be to get dinner there. But the overlooked west side of the house, bereft of landscaping or hardscaping, was another story. In Southern California a western exposure is not to be neglected. We cleared out much of the scrub brush on that side of the house and replaced it with an irrigated lawn. I next laid Arizona flagstone in an informal, irregular pattern. There is nothing as good as those Mediterranean stalwarts rosemary, lavender, and geraniums to fill dozens of terra-cotta pots to great casual and aromatic effect.

Now this west terrace is a fantastic venue for morning coffee and lounging, crowded garden parties and children's lunches, early evening cocktails and elegant candlelit dinners. Adjacent to the terrace was an outstanding wrought-iron arbor and trellis that a venerable old wisteria vine clutched onto. These things thrive in the summer under abundant violet summer shade. I set out various flea market finds and favorite old French wicker pieces. All of these outdoor rooms on the west side of the house now fully teem with sun and life. It was so much fun getting my friends together in each of the enchanting Ojai seasons.

"Kathryn lives life with all the glorious ingredients of the best things in the world. If you want a design miracle you call Kathryn. Not only will she give you the most amazing new space to live in but she will show you how do it and dance with you until dawn. Literally!"

—Ursula Brooks, actress

The front lawn facing the south patio, once cleaned up of overgrown foliage and the old rock ponds removed, created a wonderful expanse of lawn for kids and dogs to hang out and my friends to pitch their tents.

For whatever reason, a pool was never factored into the original designs for the estate by either Neff or Pierpont. But when kids are involved, a pool is a most desirable amenity. I prefer not to have the pool be the main view through inside windows, so I sited it in an area somewhat remote from the main residence, in a meadow ringed by old stone walls probably used for livestock. Imagining a pool and seeing it finally filled are always on either end of a very laborious process of construction. The finished result appears today as it might have actually looked in the 1920s and '30s if either Libbey or Lucking had chosen to install it himself.

The house and grounds were finished in time for *Vogue Living* to shoot the place. I had known Hamish Bowles, the editor, from my London days. My middle son, however, gave me a very firm deadline of how long he would be available. At one point I had to use my rather pathetic mothering tools and have a sharp word with him so that we could get the shot. I have a feeling it may have involved money!

THE LIBBEY RANCH was always intended for a great deal of entertaining; it was designed for it—horseback picnics, Fourth of July cookouts, impromptu weekend brunches, and more formal special occasions. During my time there, I got to meet Lucking's daughter-in-law, who was my neighbor living in a charming Spanish cottage across the driveway. As she walked through the property for the first time in many years, she was close to tears. The magic of the place had for some time disappeared and the laughter and entertaining that had gone on was a thing of the past. She assured me that William would have approved of my work. He bought the place as his folly, a retreat from the outside world, a place to enjoy and entertain. She and her daughter talked fondly of their memories, pointing out the stone walls they had used as jumps for their horses, reminiscing on the house parties that took place and how idyllic it was growing up there.

For me, being a mother of three, it's always been about the memories that you create for your children. I had that growing up on the west coast of Scotland, with parents who were anything but reclusive. Entertaining is in my blood. One of the distinct pleasures of living and entertaining in large houses is that convenient and comfortable split between private and public space, between the intimacy and quiet of one's own quarters and the welcome noise and company of the various shared common rooms. Everyone has enough private space to regroup and recharge so they can return with renewed energy to the party, start some sort of daube provençale in the kitchen, gather firewood or rogue blackberries, captain a squad of beachcombers and bodysurfers, or merely enjoy the latest performance by the party raconteur. The basis for all of this division of labor and mirth is just the ancient phenomenon of sharing, persuading individuals to give of themselves according to their various abilities and to take only that which they need or truly covet. This is very much how I live my life at home in France, and to the extent possible, I try to foster this sort of joyous common purpose in my interior design work and obviously in my efforts at architectural restoration. So it was sheer ecstasy working on an enchanting corner of the earth, a home I enjoyed creating.

Swatches

Page 55

Kathryn M. Ireland
"Brianza Jacquard" Natural

Fortuny "De Medic"
Red and Silver Gold

Kathryn M. Ireland
"Woven" Red

Kathryn M. Ireland
"George" Red

Page 67

Kathryn M. Ireland
"Claude" Green

Kathryn M. Ireland
"Brianza Jacquard" Tan

Kathryn M. Ireland
"Woven" Natural

Page 93

Kathryn M. Ireland
"Quilt" Red

Kathryn M. Ireland
"George" Blue

Bennison "Cochin"

Kathryn M. Ireland
"Oscar" Butterscotch

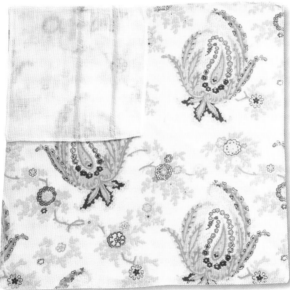

Page 99

Kathryn M. Ireland
"Paisley Stripe" Red

Kathryn M. Ireland
"Sheer Stripe" Yellow

Page 154

Robert Kime "Nine Colors"

Kathryn M. Ireland
"Woven Jacquard" Green

Kathryn M. Ireland
"Ribbed Woven" Yellow

THE Acknowledgments

There are so many to thank that I apologize if you have been forgotten. Gratitude to:

The members of my design company whose jobs went into overtime to get the house done.

Carol Ross from my office who oversaw both financial and design elements.

Jan Scott for overseeing the final months.

My brother Robert, who project managed the renovation, and his entire crew.

The friends I met in Ojai, in particular Chloe and her mum, who were the best neighbors ever.

Mel Bordeaux and Jeff Carson for helping me piece together the text.

Marc Appleton for not only writing the forward but also coming to see the project in the early days and being hugely supportive.

The fantastic photographers that helped bring the pages of this book to life.

And lastly, Madge Baird and Melissa Dymock and the Gibbs Smith team for making this book possible.

T͟H͟E͟ Photo Credits

Victoria Pearson/*House Beautiful*
Front jacket
Pages 2, 26, 27, 34, 39, 42 top and bottom, 45, 52, 55, 63, 67, 79, 86, 91, 93, 98, 101, 108, 127, 137

Dewey Nicks/*Vogue Living*
Back jacket
Pages 6, 76, 148, 155

Tim Beddow
Pages 15 top and bottom, 87, 95

Carol Ross
Pages 18, 19

Thibault Jeanson/*Vogue Living*
Pages 24, 25, 38, 80, 84, 89, 95, 111, 113, 116, 135, 140, 144, 145

Kathryn M. Ireland
Pages 28, 29, 30, 31 bottom, 80 top and bottom, 81 top right, 102, 125, 126 bottom right, 134, 136, 138 bottom left, 142 top and bottom, 143, 146, 148, 149, 152

Johanna Johnson
Page 31 top

Miguel Flores-Vianna
Pages 32 bottom, 33 top, 37, 40, 41, 43, 48, 49, 53 all, 56, 57, 58, 59, 60, 61, 62, 65, 66 bottom left, 68 top and bottom, 69, 70, 72, 73, 74, 75, 78 top, 81, 90, 96, 97, 100, 103, 104, 105, 114, 121, 122, 124, 126, 129, 130, 139

Nicholas Philp
Pages 44 all, 46 all, 47 both, 114 top and bottom, 120, 123 top and bottom, 132, 133

Michael Miller
Pages 71, 92, 106 all, 154, 155

THE Resources

KATHRYN IRELAND SHOWROOMS

Dan Marty Design
Pacific Design Center
8687 Melrose Ave., Suite B380
West Hollywood, CA 90069
310.652.6928 Tel
310.652.6923 Fax

Dorian Bahr Companies
Decorative Center Houston
5120 Woodway Dr., Suite 130
Houston, TX 77056
713.599.0900 Tel
713.599.0905 Fax

Elinor and Verve
5601 6th Ave. South
Showroom 268
Seattle, WA 98108
206.767.6941 Tel
206.767.7011 Fax

Grizzel & Mann
351 Peachtree Hills Ave., Suite 120
Atlanta, GA 30305
404.261.5932 Tel
404.261.5958 Fax

INTO
40 N. Hotel St.
Honolulu, HI 96813
808.536.2211 Tel
808.536.2266 Fax

John Brooks
2712 N. 68th St.
Scottsdale, AZ 85257
480.675.8828 Tel
480.675.7722 Fax

John Brooks
601 S. Broadway, Suite L
Denver, CO 80209
303.698.9977 Tel
303.698.9797 Fax

John Rosselli & Associates
Design Center of the Americas
1855 Griffin Rd., Suite A-128
Dania, FL 33004-2239
954.920.1700 Tel
954.920.5686 Fax

John Rosselli & Associates
6-158 Merchandise Mart
Chicago, IL 60654
312.822.0760 Tel
312.822.0764 Fax

John Rosselli & Associates
D&D Building
979 Third Ave., Suite 701
New York, NY 10022
212.593.2060 Tel
212.832.3687 Fax

John Rosselli & Associates
1515 Wisconsin Ave., NW
Washington, DC 20007
202.337.7676 Tel
202.337.4443 Fax

Kathryn Ireland
Fairbanks Studio 2
65-69 Lots Rd.
London SW10 0RN, UK
44.020.7751.4554 Tel
44.020.7751.4555 Fax

Macarena Saiz
Velazquez, 115 bajo-5
28006 Madrid, SPAIN
34.91.56.24.754 Tel
34.91.41.11.584 Fax

Mavromac (PTY) Ltd.
76178 Wendywood, Johannesburg
2144 SOUTH AFRICA
27.444.1584 Tel
27.444.1541 Fax

McRae & Co.
101 Henry Adams St.
Galleria Suite 480
San Francisco, CA 94103
415.626.2726 Tel
415.626.0262 Fax

Studio 534
One Design Center Place, Suite 534
Boston, MA 02210
617.345.9900 Tel
617.345.9910 Fax

Tigger Hall Showroom
AUSTRALIA
www.tiggerhall.com
61.3.9428.0022

ANTIQUES, FURNITURE, SOFT FURNISHINGS

Amadi Carpets
408 North Robertson Blvd.
West Hollywood, CA 90048
310.659.5353 Tel
310.652.0171 Fax
Rugs

Berbere Imports
3049 South La Cienega Blvd.
Culver City, CA 90232
310.842.3842 Tel
310.836.3225 Fax
www.berbereimports.com
Eclectic old-world imports, furniture,
garden, lighting, old-world pottery

Big Daddy
13100 South Broadway
Los Angeles, CA 90061
310.769.6600 Tel
310.769.6606 Fax
www.bdantiques.com
Antiques

Country Gear, Ltd.
2408 Main St.
PO Box 727
Bridgehampton, NY 11032
631.537.7069 Tel
631.537.6979 Fax
www.countrygearltd.com
Lloyd Loom chairs, furniture, lighting

Dan Marty Designs
8687 Melrose Ave., Ste. B380
West Hollywood, CA 90069
310.652.6928 Tel
310.652.6923 Fax
www.danmartydesigns.com
Eclectic antiques, antique
finds, vintage textiles

Eccola Eclectic
8569 Higuera St.
Culver City, CA 90232
310.839.2244 Tel
Furniture

Elson Rugs
3723 Sacramento St.
San Francisco, CA 94118
800.944.2858 Tel
202.333.7120 Tel
www.elsoncompany.com
Rugs

Europa
2345 Lillie Ave.
Summerland, CA 93067
805.969.4989 Tel
805.969.5605 Fax
Furniture, rare art

J. Roaman
48 Newtown Ln.
East Hampton, NY 11937
631.329.0662 Tel
www.jroaman.com
Eclectic furniture

Jewel Box
3100 Wilshire Blvd.
Santa Monica, CA 90403
www.jewelboxframes.com
Framing, photos, accessories

John Robshaw
245 W. 29th St., Ste. 1501
New York, NY 10001
212.594.6006 Tel
212.594.6166 Fax
www.johnrobshaw.com
Bedding

Kathryn Ireland Home
1714 18th St.
Santa Monica, CA 90404
310.399.0300 Tel
310.399.8787 Fax
www.kathrynireland.com
Custom furniture, lamps,
pillows, tables, chairs

Lief
646 North Almont Dr.
Los Angeles, CA 90069
310.492.0033 Tel
310.492.0026 Fax
www.liefaa.com
Furniture, objets d'art, paintings

Louise Fletcher
Decorative Paintings
1520 S. Campe Ave.
Los Angeles, CA 90025
310.477.5049 Tel
Art

Rosemarie McCaffrey Antiques
1203 Montana Ave.
Santa Monica, CA 90403
310.395.7711 Tel
310.395.5667 Fax
www.rmantique.com
Furniture, lighting

Michael Haskell Antiques
539 San Ysidro Rd.
Montecito, CA 93108
805.565.1121 Tel
805.565.1541 Fax
Spanish colonial antiquities, accessories

Nathan Turner Antiques
636 N. Almont Dr.
Los Angeles, CA 90069
310.275.1209 Tel
www.nathanturner.com
Furniture, garden, accessories

Oasis
3931 S. Topanga Canyon Blvd.
Malibu, CA 90265
310.456.9883 Tel
www.oasisfurniture.net
Outdoor furniture, eco-friendly

Robert Kime
PO Box 454
Marlborough, Wiltshire
SN8 3UR, UK
020.7229.0886 Tel
www.robertkime.com
Fabrics

Rooms and Gardens
924 State St.
Santa Barbara, CA 93101
805.965.2424 Tel
805.965.2755 Fax
www.roomsandgardens.com
Furniture, bedding, pillows, accessories

Santa Barbara Mattresses
909-A De La Vina St.
Santa Barbara, CA 93101
805.962.9776 Tel
www.santabarbaramattress.com
Mattresses

William Laman
1496 East Valley Rd.
805.969.2840 Tel
805.969.2869 Fax
www.williamlaman.com
Furniture, garden, accessories

Woodwright Furniture
309 Palm Ave.
Santa Barbara, CA 93103
805.962.3551 Tel
Custom furniture

HARDWARE,
FIXTURES, LIGHTING,
PAINT, STONE, TILE

Bay City Kitchens and Appliances
1302 Santa Monica Blvd.
Santa Monica, CA 90404
310.393.3771 Tel
310.393.4933 Fax
www.baycities.net
Appliances

Bourget Brothers
1636 11th St.
Santa Monica, CA 90404
310.450.6556 Tel
www.bourgetbros.com
Gravel, stone

Farrow and Ball
1054 Yonge St.
Toronto, ONT, Canada
888.511.1121 Tel
www.farrow-ball.com
Interior/exterior paint

House of Mosaic
32 West 22nd St.
New York, NY 10010
212.414.2525 Tel
212.414.2526 Fax
www.mosaichse.com
Antique and custom tile

Liz's Hardware
453 S. La Brea Ave.
Los Angeles, CA 90036
323.939.4403 Tel
www.lahardware.com
Knobs, handles, hardware

Malibu Tile works
23852 Pacific Coast Hwy.
Malibu, CA 90265
310.456.0777 Tel
310.317.8453 Fax
www.malibutileworks.com
Custom and mosaic tile

McKinney and Co.
Studio P
The Old Imperial Laundry
71 Warriner Gardens
Battersea, London SW11 4XW, UK
44.020.7627.5077 Tel
www.mckinneydirect.co.uk
Knobs

Restoration Hardware
1221 3rd Street Promenade
Santa Monica, CA 90401
310.458.7992 Tel
Hardware, paint, bedding

Siegfried Ironworks
661.944.4493 Tel
Ironwork

Vaughan Ltd.
G1, Chelsea Harbour
Design Center
Chelsea Harbour
London SW10 0XE, UK
UK Sales 44.020.7349.4600 Tel
Export Sales 44.020.7349.4601 Tel
44.020.7349.4615 Fax
Lighting

Waterworks
60 Backus Ave.
Danbury, CT 06810
800.899.6757 Tel
800.927.2120 Technical Assistance
www.waterworks.com
Bath fixtures

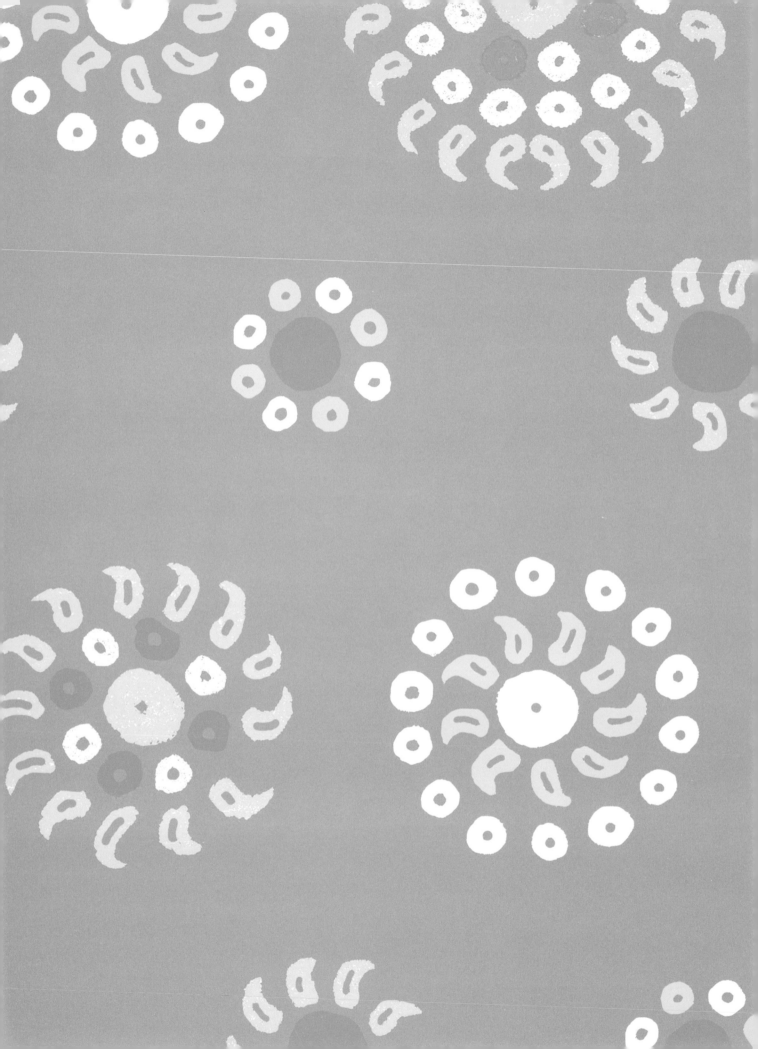